Teachah Don't Know Nothin'

Dee Oglesby

Everett Library Queens University
1900 Selwyn Ave., Charlotte, NC 28274

To the children in Chicago's schools who so graciously and generously taught me about life in the inner city.

Foreword

I met Dee Oglesby when a student in one of my classes, who had been substitute teaching at a detention center in Chicago, asked me to invite her to talk to our class. He had observed her at work and couldn't believe how enthusiastic, creative, and caring she was with her students. The detention center was a hard place to work because the student population was transient and children were not interested in learning. In Dee's class, things were different.

When Dee came to talk to my class, we didn't know what to expect. To our surprise, the lady visiting was a beautiful, conservative Southern lady. When she started talking about her job in the detention center we were captivated immediately by her stories about teaching there. She said she had decided she needed to learn about the children's lives in order to teach them. Knowing the students allowed her to plan educational activities relevant to them. She showed the university students some of her students' written work. Some of it included gang signs and graffiti. Much of it involved stories about the students' home life and street life, and about the offenses that landed them in the detention center. Some of the stories were crude and shocking. The university students asked Dee whether it was fair or educational for her to allow that type of writing. Dee explained that her method was a way for students to find functions for writing and to get them excited about literacy. She found that students who remained in her class for a long period of time did other types of writing as well. It was important, she said, for the students to connect to their own words, in order for them to come to the enjoyment of reading and writing.

Subsequently, I visited her class a number of times. Her teaching environment was not an easy one. From the beginning of her assignment to the detention center school, Dee collected student writings and made books for them to read. She organized them by topics and typed the papers so the students saw themselves as published writers. While visiting her class, I found different activities going on: one group doing art, another writing stories, others reading to their classmates from newspapers or books. A few couldn't write, but they dictated their stories to Dee who transcribed them and then they could read them.

These were students who would not read or write when they first came to Dee's classroom. What did Dee do that made the students change their attitudes toward learning and literacy? She allowed them to tell or write their own stories. They found their voices and wanted to be heard. They also wanted to read other students' stories and, from these, found a desire to learn about the world, a world beyond their neighborhood and their personal, troubled lives.

As time passed, Dee shared with me her collections of songs and rhymes from the city's neighborhood schools where she had worked previously. I also read the on-going life story of a student from the group home who kept asking Dee for paper, envelopes and stamps so that she would be able to send her writings to Dee after she left the group home. Through the years, Dee also collected a dictionary of slang and gang terms used by her students.

Teachers like Dee need to be understood. Her work could be taken as a way to keep poor, inner city children within the boundaries of their community and their experiences, but that was not her purpose. And as she taught her students she was also learning from them. She was not judgmental of what the students shared about their homes or community. Instead she used what she learned about them as a steppingstone to enhance their literacy development and their view of the world.

She understood that their lives were different from her own, that they were accustomed to a different language and culture. Her students' language seemed obscene initially, but it was just normal speech for them.

I hope that the stories in this book are understood in terms of Dee's commitment to teach all children by encouraging them to connect with their own life experiences. What made Dee a successful teacher with children very different from her was her desire to learn from them. She was also a tireless worker, as she made it possible for her students to see their words published and read. Dee was a trustful and caring teacher. Her students learned to be better people in her classrooms.

Flora Rodriquez-Brown, Professor, College of Education, University of Illinois at Chicago. Director. FLAME, an Academic Excellence project and a national model to train parents of young children how they can sustain literacy learning at home so children get ready for the transition to school.

Introduction

My initial fascination with the inner city culture can perhaps be explained by the acute difference between my background and that of my students. I came to the setting described in this book through a chain of circumstances that left me seeking employment after the school year began, when the only available job was in a black inner city school.

I needed work, so agreed to the assignment, figuring that I could stick it out for seven months and then return to work in a suburban school. Friends and professional acquaintances warned me, saying work in the inner city was too dangerous, but I had to have work and teaching was the only work I knew. My initial shock was too enormous for description.

I grew up in a zealous religious atmosphere in a small cotton mill community in North Carolina. My family attended the Church of God Sunday mornings, Sunday evenings, and Wednesday evenings and often for other events. Social activities were church-related. Included on the list of sins were sports, dancing, movies, jewelry, make-up, shorts and slacks (for females), and swear words. No work except cooking the midday meal was allowed on Sunday. We couldn't sew on a button or mend a hem on a dress to wear to church - and certainly no shopping on Sunday. We couldn't smoke or drink any day of the week. When my mother decided she had too much work to do to attend church, the minister and deacons came to our home to pray the devil out of her.

At school I was still in the midst of a Christian world. All the students in the public school were Caucasian, Protestant, and Bible classes were part of the curriculum.

I knew very little about people who believed anything different, knew nothing about other cultures except what I picked up from reading. In seventh grade, a Catholic family moved to town and the teacher had the student stand before the class and tell us about the Catholic Church.

In my church, Catholics were not considered Christians. We were taught to believe they were the most sinful of people, going to hell because they believed in the Pope instead of Jesus. Jews ranked a little higher, but still were going to hell because they killed Jesus. Then came blacks, not going to hell, but could not be a real part of our world. They only worked for white people, and went back to their own world. I didn't think to wonder if God prepared separate parts of heaven.

I was more observant of the church's teachings than most of my peers. If I rebelled, I chewed gum in church or went roller-skating. By age twelve, I was teaching Sunday school, cleaning the church, helping to organize and produce special programs, and singing in the choir. In 1944, I graduated from high school with no real goal except to continue church work. I became state director of Children's work and secretary for the state Ministerial Association.

My religious beliefs changed after I left my small community, but my morals remained the same and exposure to other cultures remained minimal. Getting thrown into an inner city school was like getting baptized in the river. I came up drenched, shaking myself in bewilderment. Very soon, though, I discovered to my amazement that I loved my new job.

My friends asked how I could possibly enjoy going into the ghettos to work. They said I had to be trying to punish myself. One friend had a very strong reaction. She said "we" had spent enough trying to help "them," that the best solution would be to bomb the entire area "so we could live in peace."

Most people, I soon learned, simply ignored the ghetto sections of our society - or pretended they didn't exist. An editorial in the *Chicago Tribune* called gang members "renegade mutants."

I came to know some of those "mutants," and discovered they were human beings who wanted to believe they could live the American Dream, like everyone else.

Most of the children in this book were wrong because they were born. They learned early that a life of crime is a route to reward. Yes, crime often means risking life, but a life with no future loses nothing when it ends.

These kids say, this is who we are, this is the way we think, and the way we live. They tell us in poems, stories, plays, and in conversations on the recorder I set down in their midst. With older students I also taped interviews.

This book was made from those saved materials and notes. Some of the incidents may be assigned to a different school from where they actually happened because of lapses in memory and omissions in notes. The story includes the years 1971 through 1993.

Dee Oglesby
Summer 2000

Chapter One

I wondered why a policeman was standing at the top of the steps at Haven School. Did all Chicago schools have police guards? Why was a white policeman sent to guard a black school?

He leaned toward me with a questioning look on his face that said, "What are you doing here?"

"I'm the new kindergarten teacher," I said in answer to his unspoken question.

"You mean you're going to teach in *this* school?"

As he held the door for me, he said, "Honey, you don't know what you're in for. This is a high crime area. All the mothers are prostitutes. If you last a year in this school, you'll have done your penance for a lifetime."

Penance? The word rolled around in my head like marbles as I walked into the building. What was penance? Oh, I thought, that's something Catholics do to pay for sins.

Teachah Don't Know Nothin'

Although the lights were on in the school, the two-story-high entryway was dark and smelled musty. The click-clack of my footsteps echoed. In my classroom I discovered old tables with old chairs that looked like they'd been salvaged from a dumpster. The room was on the first floor and enormous, big enough to hear echoes. I walked over to the dingy windows and looked at an alleyway and the brick wall of an auto repair shop.

Noise from the nearby elevated train was so deafening I wanted to cover my ears. On a beat-up wooden bookshelf I found discarded books from the upper grades, a stack of construction paper, and a box of broken crayons. An empty sand box lay in the corner, and nearby a few broken toys.

What was I doing here? In the suburban schools where I was used to working, everything a teacher needed or wanted was provided. Well, I thought, I only have to put up with this place for the remainder of the year. I will survive.

Like the rest of the furniture, my desk was scarred and battered. The previous teacher had left the attendance book in the center of the desk where I'd be sure to find it. I wondered why she had left, a job in a better school maybe? Or was she unable to handle the children?

I put one of the chairs in front of the chalkboard and placed the attendance book on the seat along with a storybook I found on the shelf. I was ready.

The students ran in noisily and headed for the coatroom. This wasn't their first day. It was a cold day in November, and my first day.

The policeman had said this was a high-crime area, but the children looked well cared for. Their clothing was

Chapter One

appropriate for the weather, and most of the children were clean and attractive. The girls' hair was either braided or neatly combed, and the boys' hair cut short.

As they came from the coatroom, I directed them to sit on the floor in front of my chair. One of the girls said, "I ain't gonna sit on dat dirty flo."

The floor had been swept, but did look dirty. "OK, let's get the chairs," I said. (Later I found a pretty rug for the floor.) We made a circle of twenty chairs. I sat in front of the kids and thought I'd start by helping them pronounce my name. I said Mrs. Oglesby. They said Ogleby or Mis' Oglebill, and other pronunciations. They just couldn't seem to pronounce the *s*. We settled for "teachah."

Then came roll call. Each child raised a hand and said "Heah," until I came to the name "Termesia." They looked around at each other. "We ain't got nobody like dat in heah." I kept trying to find other ways to pronounce the name. Ter-me-si-a, that was the name, but how else could I pronounce it? Lisa, the girl who had refused to sit on the floor, grinned. She was a pretty, light-skinned girl with big eyes. Her eyes lit up as she said, "She mean Ka-me-sha, yawl!"

"Ka-me-sha, Ka-me-sha," they began chanting, all of them together saying "Ka-me-sha." And the chant didn't stop. I joined in, gradually slowed down the volume and tempo, then swung my arm up and down to my knees and stopped it.

If another chant started, would I be able to stop it in the same way? I began counting the children aloud. When I got to "five" someone interrupted. "She mean fi-ive, yawl."

Teachah Don't Know Nothin'

Hard as I tried, I couldn't pronounce five with such a flattened "i."

They only knew one of the songs I named, "Mary Had a Little Lamb." We sang that a few times, then I taught them a few songs and rhymes. "Now, do you have any songs you'd like to sing?"

The talker in the group, Lisa, in a fancy pink dress with a ruffled skirt, came up and whispered in my ear. "We can sing 'The General.'"

I put my arm around her and told her to start. She did, and the others joined in to the tune of "Honey, Baby, Mine."

> The General made some black-eyed peas,
> honey, honey,
> The General made some black-eyed peas, hey.
> The General made some black-eyed peas,
> Somebody pissed in his good peas,
> Honey, oh, baby, mine.

Had I heard correctly? "What did somebody do in the General's peas?" I asked.

"Pissed! Pissed! Don't you know what dat mean? It mean peed, peed! Somebody peed in the General's peas!" I did know what pissed meant, but I'd never heard it in a song, certainly not in a song sung by children in school.

Melvin, a tall skinny boy, one of the few shabbily dressed, came up. "We can sing, 'Ain't yo Mama Pretty.'" He started and the rest joined in.

> Hey, hey, ain't yo mama pretty.
> She got ham and eggs
> Between her legs.

Chapter One

> Hey, hey, ain't yo mama pretty.
> We took her to a party,
> She turned around and farted.
> Hey, hey, ain't yo mama pretty.

What was going on here? I didn't know children knew songs like that and couldn't believe they were singing them in school the same way they'd sung "Mary had a Little Lamb." The children, though, were having a great time. Ivory, a big husky boy who had begun the school day by racing into the room and sliding across the floor, said, "Let's sing 'James Brown.' "

> James Brown, got the beat,
> In the bushes you must go
> In the bushes on the flo.
> Won't your mama be surprised
> When she see yo belly rise,
> Won't your daddy be disgusted
> When he know your cherry busted.
> Won't your uncle be ashamed
> When he know that he to blame.

My southern reserve had not prepared me for this. I was embarrassed. When I was their age I didn't know such words, and when I did learn them I certainly didn't say them out loud.

I held in the shock that was ricocheting inside me like a ball in a racquetball court. I said, "Do you know any religious songs? Spirituals? Songs you sing in church?"

"Church?" Mary said. " We don't go to church. Dat's not the fad."

Time to read a story.

Teachah Don't Know Nothin'

The kids sat in a semi-circle around me, listening attentively, but every few minutes an el train passed. All the trains going south passed within about ten feet of the back of the building, and we were near the back. The noise was horrendous and constant and seemed to shake the building. I had to pause repeatedly, and was surprised that the children waited patiently for the noise to subside. During the day, I noticed that when a train passed the children either yelled to each other over the noise or stopped talking until the noise ceased, never seeming to lose track of what they were saying or getting the least bit upset.

Melvin pointed to a picture of a cow in the book I was reading, "What's dat?"

"A cow," I answered.

"Do dem tawk?"

"They make a sound like 'moooo.' "

"On TV dey tawk."

Another child asked, "Ain't dis a horse?"

"No," said Ivory, "dat's a turtle." It was really a brown rabbit.

"What's dat pig doin' dare?" It was a cow being milked.

Vanessa, one of the smallest children, hunched her shoulders and said, "I wouldn't be a pig and let folks yank on me like dat."

Lisa said, "Is a cow biggah den a pig?"

Lincoln Park Children's Zoo was one short bus ride away. Obviously these children had never been there. I wondered if they had ever left their buildings on 18th and

Chapter One

Wabash to go any farther than the school on 14th and Wabash.

During playtime Ivory raced around the room, bumping into other children and generally causing havoc. I pulled him to a chair and sat down with him. He said, "You rich, teachah? All white people's rich."

"No, Ivory, I'm not rich." If I'd been rich I wouldn't have been there with him.

As we sat at the tables having juice and crackers, Mary, the only child whose skin was deep black, spilled juice on Lisa's frilly pink dress. Lisa jumped up, rubbing on the dress, almost in tears, "My Mamma worked for dis dress! My Mamma worked for dis dress!"

A strange thing to say, I thought. People usually worked for what they had. I later learned that "to work" meant to work at prostitution.

Lisa slapped Mary. I put my arm around Lisa to calm her down. She screamed, "Mary said da men don't like my mothah!"

"Lisa," I said, "I'm sure everybody likes your mother. She must be as pretty as you are."

I turned around in time to grab the chair Ivory had over his head ready to slam down on Mary. He yelled, "She was talkin' about my mothah!'"

"What did she say about your mother?"

"She said, 'Yo mama.'"

"Oh, then, she didn't really say anything about your mother. She just started to say something and didn't finish it."

21

Teachah Don't Know Nothin'

"She did talk about my mothah! She did talk about my mothah!"

I led him away from Mary and got him quiet, but I didn't understand. It was three years later in another school with older children that I learned the meaning of 'yo mama.'

During playtime Lisa and one of the other girls threw their hands in the air and rolled on the floor. Lisa said, "Heah, ovah heah, sistah. Take care of dis chile. She got da Holy Ghost." Maybe church wasn't the fad, but they had some contact with church.

While looking for something in the drawer of my desk, I found a piece of peppermint candy and laid it on the desk top. A chubby girl in a polka-dot skirt named Vanessa noticed it. She asked, "Dat yourn?"

I said, "You should say, 'is that yours?'"

"Dat's mine!" she said as she grabbed the candy and popped it into her mouth.

The lunchroom was down the hallway on the opposite side of the school. I lined the children up by twos. Just as they got outside the door, one of the boys started singing "Miss Mary Mac, Mac, Mac," and the others joined in. They sang and danced down the hall. I knew they wouldn't hear me if I called to them, so I ran to the front of the line and quieted them before we got to the lunchroom.

During lunch, Lisa, who was sitting next to me, looked at her plate, pointed to some food and asked, "What's dat?"

"Oh, that's baked beans." I *did* know that. All morning I'd been exposed to a culture I knew nothing about, but I *did* know what baked beans were.

Chapter One

She took a little taste and announced to the class, "Dat's not baked beans, yawl, dem's poke-n-beans. Teachah don't know nothin'."

Chapter Two

A half-hour play period was scheduled after lunch when the kids went outside. On days when the weather was bad, I had them. About fifty children showed up in the kindergarten room. (Kindergartners went home after lunch.) Two teacher-aides came in and brought a TV. Even so, after the first session the room looked like a bunch of looters had ransacked the place.

The second day I hid things I didn't want used, and got kids in front of the TV as they came in, seated on chairs, tables and window ledges. I was standing by the TV near the door when from a small group of boys in the far corner of the room I heard chanting. I found my way through the children and said to the boys, "Say it again. I'd like to hear it. Stand on the table so others can hear it, too."

They grinned at each other, stood on the table, and began:

Teachah Don't Know Nothin'

 Rev-o-lu-tion, rev-o-lu-tion,
People movin' out, people movin' in,
All because of the color of the skin.
Re-vo-lu-tion, re-vo-lu-tion,
Say it loud, black and proud.

Hands began popping up all over the room. "Let me do one." Soon everybody was involved with performing and TV was forgotten.

A group of sixth-graders sang the following to the tune of "Dem Bones," an old Negro spiritual.

Now, the Lord, he thought he'd make a man,
So he took a little water and he took a little sand,
But Adam, he was so powerful blue,
He didn't know quite what to do.
So the Lord took a rib from Adam's side
And gave him Miss Eve to be his bride.
He put them in a garden fair
And thought they'd be most happy there.
Peaches, pears, plums and such,
But of that tree you must not touch.
Around that tree old Satan slunk
And at Miss Eve his eye he wunk.
"Miss Eve, them apples is mighty fine,
Take just one, the Lord won't mind."
So she took a little peck and she took a little pull
And soon she filled her apron full.
The next day when the Lord came down,
He spied them cores all over the ground.
"Adam, Adam, where art thou?"
"Here I is, Lord. I'm comin' right now."

Chapter Two

"Adam, who these cores did leave?"
"Twern't me, Lord. 'Spect was Eve."
"Adam, you must leave this place
And earn your livin' by the sweat of your face."
So Eve took a hoe and Adam took a plow,
And that's why we're all working now.
That's all there is, there ain't no more,
'Cause Eve got the apple, and Adam got the core.
The moral of this story be,
Don't leave them cores where the Lord can see.

Between each line they sang "Dem bones gonna rise again." Between each two lines, they sang the chorus: "I know, know it, indeed I know it, brother, I know it, whee, dem bones gonna rise again."

Lunchtime became "Show Time." We all had fun, and I'd found a way to preserve my classroom.

Soon we decided to have a talent show and invite families. Mr. Breen, the principal, liked the idea. Children chose their own rhymes, songs, and dances, and although I was a little concerned about some of the appropriateness of the language, I didn't censor. It was their show.

The boys who started it all usually stayed behind to help me straighten the room. They talked excitedly and made plans for their performance. They wanted a name for their group and quickly decided on one: The Three Pimps.

"Are you sure it's Pimps?" I asked as I wrote it down. "I think you might mean Pips."

"Nope, The Three Pimps." That was firm.

Pimp was a word I'd heard but wasn't used to using. I thought a pimp was a man who had a group of girls he managed for prostitution. If the mothers were prostitutes, as I'd been told, maybe the boys did mean pimps. I wrote "The Three Pimps" on the program, thinking Mr. Breen would remove it. He didn't.

A group of ten seventh and eighth grade girls practiced their talent show act at home. One afternoon at school they asked me to watch their dance. They moved the desks and chairs to one side in the eighth grade room and put a record on the record player to "dance off."

They lined themselves up and began. I had never seen anything like it. Their movements were all as one, with fast steps and slow steps, similar to Scottish Highland dancers, and they moved their arms like eagle wings. Their skips and jumps seemed to be done with total abandon, as though there was no thought involved, yet they all moved together. Their faces were a delight to see, bright with joy and laughter. The sight was more beautiful than ballets I'd seen in theaters. Tears rolled down my cheeks.

For all my years of teaching, including years of working with church groups, when preparing for performances, I selected the material, chose the children for the various parts, and directed the performance - a totally teacher-directed enterprise. I'd never thought children could plan and perform their own program.

Here I sat, watching girls produce to perfection complicated dance steps. When one girl stepped out of line, or they decided to change a step, they did it themselves. Yes, I was overwhelmed: by the sheer beauty of the dance, and by the impact of what I was learning from these kids.

Chapter Two

The children were always chewing and popping gum. When I asked one of the teachers she confirmed what I suspected, children were not supposed to be chewing gum at school. During practice one afternoon, I watched the ever-moving gum-filled mouths and told the children I thought it was not appropriate for them to chew gum during the program. I made a rule: no gum chewing during the show.

Mr. Breen had the third floor gym room inspected and found it was safe enough for our program to be held there. The building was so old and in such poor condition that the upper two floors were not used.

Jerry, the loudest and most aggressive of the boys, took over the job of program announcer. As I walked up the stairs with him on show day, he looked behind him and said, "I's the pro-nouncer of dis show. Now, all you little kids stay behind yo fathah and yo mothah!" I grinned and took hold of his arm.

I had imagined the children and parents coming in quiet and orderly as in suburban schools. Instead, it was like a picnic, everyone talking loudly, laughing, and calling to each other. I looked around the room and said to the teacher-aide sitting beside me, "Mrs. Shelton, everyone in here is chewing gum!"

"I know," she said, "and I forgot mine." Someone passed some to her. Everyone seemed to enjoy the gum so much I wanted to ask for some for myself. The children had treated my no-gum-chewing rule as children usually treat adult rules they don't like: they ignored it. After that day I

Teachah Don't Know Nothin'

practiced trying to pop gum the way they did. Never could do it.

We'd borrowed the microphone and a good record player from the Board of Education. Jerry said into the microphone loud enough to be heard over the commotion, "I's the pro-nouncer of dis show. Now it's time to start the show."

The children had gone to their relatives and friends, instead of staying with their groups. Everyone was visiting with everyone else as if this were a holiday. Even the General who made some black-eyed peas was in the audience. That's when I learned he was a real person.

I watched Mr. Breen closely as the kindergartners sang "The General" and "James Brown." Their singing was followed by lots of clapping and cheers, and Mr. Breen didn't seem to pay any attention to the words.

I thought I'd allowed plenty of time for the performances, but children had to be gathered from all over the room and time seemed unimportant to anyone. We were running late. I was wondering if we could continue a few minutes past the usual school-closing time, since all the children walked home, when Mr. Breen stood up and announced that the program was over.

The junior high girls didn't get to perform their wonderful dance. I thought, oh my goodness, what are we going to do now? I expected a riot. I looked across the room at the girls, dressed in their yellow and red dance outfits. They were slumped in their seats and merely looked disappointed. But I was angry - we could have stayed ten minutes longer.

Chapter Two

Later that day as we were going down the stairs, Mr. Breen said, "Mrs. Oglesby, your program worked out well. However, I think you could have been more careful and not allowed them to do those suggestive dances." I couldn't imagine what he meant by "suggestive dances" since all the dances had been performed by young children. I'd expected him to make some comment about the words to their songs.

"What are we going to do about the dance the older girls were going to do?" I asked him. "They practiced long and hard, and bought special costumes. We can't leave it like this, you know."

He stood at the bottom of the stairs and stared at the floor before he answered, but he agreed. "We'll talk about it in the morning." The next morning we made plans for a family night, a PTA meeting, with the girls' dance to be the main attraction. I was at the door with the good news when the girls arrived for school that morning. Not only could they perform, they could perform more than one dance. Happy girls danced down the hall to their classroom.

Chapter Three

Mornings I was a kindergartner teacher. Afternoons I gave tests to older students, a position called Adjustment Teacher. One day I was looking at some citywide achievement tests I'd given when Mrs. Shelton, the teacher-aide, came in. She was a heavy-set woman, maybe 30 or 35, who lived in one of the two buildings that housed the children. "Mrs. Shelton," I said, "I'm concerned about these test scores. The children don't read the questions, they just mark answers."

Mrs. Shelton looked at one of the tests and said, "What do you expect? Just look at this question. How many kids would know that a can'-er-y is a bird?"

I kept a straight face and made no comment on her pronunciation. I learned from Mr. Hawkins, the assistant principal, a big, pleasant, handsome black man, that in the history of Haven School only one student had graduated

Teachah Don't Know Nothin'

high school. The students began freshman year, but before the year was over the girls usually got pregnant and the boys took to the streets.

The third-grade teacher told me she used to send the worst readers for special reading help. Then she found the students could only be one or two years behind, with an I.Q. of 85 or above, so she started sending her best students for extra help.

None of the tests I administered were within the achievement level of any of the kids in the school. Even if they could read the words, the words had no meaning for them. Sometimes their haphazard way of marking answers gave them scores higher than their real achievement levels.

I decided to try a different tactic with the eighth-graders. I told them they were "specially chosen for this questionnaire."

One of the boys asked, "Who decided for us to do dis?"

"Oh, you were specially chosen," I answered.

"I'm gonna tell my mothah that da President of the United States asked me to do dis."

Scores were higher on that test. They spent more time with the questions.

When I went to the fourth grade teacher for a test score on one of the students, she said, "Won't matter anyhow, she's so low. She's below the average here, does bottom-of-the-bucket work."

I was beginning to think all the children at Haven School were considered bottom-of the-bucket children, yet I knew their I.Q. scores were no more accurate than the achievement test scores. They understood directions, they

Chapter Three

were enthusiastic, and could communicate. People didn't expect them to achieve, so they believed they couldn't.

I wanted to get a feeling for the area where the children lived and occasionally drove by their buildings before going home. One afternoon I drove down Wabash and was nearing 18th Street when I heard glass breaking behind me. In the rearview mirror I saw people fighting in the middle of the street.

Making a quick turn onto 18th, I got out of there. Heading back toward the Loop, I heard the sirens of police cars rushing south. Television news that night reported that three men had been killed and many others injured.

The next day talkative Lisa told the story. "Sally Dee messed wif de black store man. She smart wif her ole fat sef. De store man hit her and broke her bottle o' wine and her boyfriend got mad."

I asked, "What did you do when it happened, Lisa?"

She squared her shoulders and said, "One a dem men started to mess wif my mothah and I said, 'Look heah man, you don't know who you messin' wif if you mess wif my mothah.'"

I stared at Lisa. How could that pretty little round-faced girl have shown that kind of spunk?

Later in the day Lisa said, "I want my money." I kept money children brought to school and returned it at the end of the day.

"Yes, Lisa, when it's time to go home."

35

Teachah Don't Know Nothin'

She put her hands on her hips, stared at me, and said in a very determined voice, "I said, I want my money."

"When it's time to go home, Lisa."

She propped her elbows on the table, squinted her eyes, and said in a quiet tone that sounded threatening, "I - said - I - want - my - money!" Yes, Lisa would have been in the middle of the riot and would have looked any man in the eye and told him not to mess with her mama.

She was exceptionally pretty, with large dark eyes and a spicy personality. Her sister, Jackie, in the eighth grade, was just as cute with a similar personality. One afternoon I went to the library to supervise the junior high students who were waiting for a speaker. They were seated in a semi-circle, and orderly. I slid into an empty chair near the door. After a few minutes I heard, in a loud voice behind me, "Get yo fat sef ovah heah, you mothahfucker."

My head jerked around and there sat Jackie. Her hand covered her mouth when she saw me. "Oh, my God," she gasped.

"Don't worry, Jackie," I said. "I'll pretend I didn't hear anything."

"Oh, thanks, Mrs. Ogleby. You sure saved my ass."

I laughed. Jackie's use of ass didn't work, and neither did her Oh, my God. I began wondering what makes words acceptable or not acceptable. What makes a word a swear word?

Where I grew up, 'hell' was a swear word unless it was used to mean the opposite of heaven. At school in seventh grade, I once said 'darn' and thought I'd sinned. Same thing happened as an adult: As I drove home from school one

Chapter Three

afternoon, in my thoughts I said 'damn.' I looked over to the empty seat beside me and said, "Sorry, Mama, I'm learning to swear."

After Christmas that year Jackie added to the picture I was getting of the lives of the children. As she walked by the kindergarten room, I asked, "How was your Christmas, Jackie?"

"Not good. I spent it in the hospital with my mothah. She got stabbed wif a knife."

"Oh," I said, "I hope they caught the person who did it."

Jackie said, "No, he was in the hospital wif me. He was my mothah's boyfriend."

Soon after that, as my kindergartners were getting ready for story time, Lori twisted her long straightened hair and said to me, "My sistah seen a man in a windah. He was holdin' on dat line, and he said to tell Corrine to tell her mothah to look at him. Den he jumped out dat windah."

Lisa spoke up. "When we wus goin' on 18th Street fo to get some milk, dat man jumped out da third flo. When you be dead, dat be good fo you. He was drivin' in a ambulance, but he not dead. He cut his feet with no shoes on."

Lori said, "He was my mothah's friend."

Mary said, "He was my mothah's friend."

The children liked to talk about the men who came to see their mothers. During lunch one day Lisa said, "My mama's friend got us Kentucky Fried Chicken, hamburgers, some French fries, and some pop. Boy, it was good! I don't know his name, but all the men like my mothah."

Vanessa wasn't to be left out. She flipped her chin up and said to Lisa, "All the men like my mothah, and the women,

Teachah Don't Know Nothin'

too. Women don't like yo mothah. Yo mothah haf to git de broom to fight wif."

I asked, "Vanessa, does your father like for the men to come see your mother?"

"Cose he do."

"Do any white men come to see your mother?"

"Sho do," she said. "My white fathah."

The policeman at the door on my first day had said the mothers were all prostitutes. Maybe he was right.

Chapter Four

The two big dilapidated apartment buildings where the children lived sat on the east side of a broken-down business area at 18th and Wabash. Stairways opened to the sidewalk, which was their playground. Many windows were cracked and taped together, or broken and covered with cardboard. The sidewalks and streets were littered with trash.

The children talked about where they lived as their "house" where they "stayed." The word "home" was not used, and they never used the word "live" to mean where they lived. "Where you stay?" was said to mean "Where do you live?"

As the children talked about where they lived they made many comments such as these:

"Rats come outa de hole every time I went to the bedroom and the kitchen."

Teachah Don't Know Nothin'

"Every time I kicked the doh shut somebody broke in."

"Somebody cut off the heat and the water and it was cold in the house. We gets in the bed and cover with blankets and keeps us warm."

"The day he slept in the bed his father pulled him outa de bed and put him on the flo and then put him out the doh. His mother started crying and he couldn't come back so he had to run away."

One of the jump rope rhymes speaks about their homes:

Fudge, fudge, a boom, boom,
Love that job, boom, boom, boom.
Mama got a new born baby, boom, boom,
Daddy's going crazy, boom, boom.
First flo was Miss Allen's house,
Second flo was Miss Kenny's,
Third flo was Miss Simmons' house,
Fourth flo was Miss Williams'.
Fudge, fudge, fudge, a boom, boom.

At first I thought words for rhymes were picked because they rhymed, not because of meaning. I found that was seldom true. Everything had a meaning. Maybe not a meaning the kids were aware of, but a real meaning. In one rhyme that said, "Yo mama got the measles and yo daddy got the pox," measles and pox were names for venereal diseases.

Toward the end of the school year Mr. Breen said there would be time during the summer months for testing any children who were slow mentally or seemed to have learning problems. I made a list for the school that included three boys from the kindergarten class

Chapter Four

One afternoon Ivory's grandmother, Melvin's mother, and the General came in the classroom very distraught. They talked and I listened. I learned that the General was the neighborhood patriarch. People listened to him and seemed to think he knew everything. In his late fifties or early sixties, with graying hair, he was a distinguished-looking black man.

He said, "Mis' Shelton said you got Ivory, Kenny and Melvin on a list for the dumb room. We want to know where you gonna have this dumb room and who gonna teach it."

Ivory's grandmother said, "If you ain't got no teachah for the dumb room, the General could teach it. He know how to teach the children."

The General leaned forward and laid his bony hand on the table. He looked me in the eye and said in a smooth, quiet voice, "We want Head Start for our children so they can learn to read when they three and four years old. Besides, we know they ain't dumb, 'cause dumb means they can't hear, and we know they can hear, so what kind of dumb room you gonna have?"

I was dumbfounded. How could I explain to these people about an educational procedure? How could I help them know there was to be no dumb room? I knew Kenny and Melvin had older siblings in the E.M.H. Room (Educable Mentally Handicapped), and I also knew they were not retarded.

I explained about the tests that were to be administered, that the tests would help teachers know how best to work

Teachah Don't Know Nothin'

with the children. Before the three left they agreed that the children could take the tests.

I was impressed with the General. He told me about a marching band he had started for the children. Sometime soon after that my husband and I were at the Art Institute and spotted a children's band going down the other side of Michigan Avenue.

I recognized the General and some of my students and rushed over to speak to them.

The General led the band, but his band had no instruments except built-in ones: hands, feet, and voices. I was surprised at how young the children were, between five and eight years old. They wore colorful uniforms, yellow and red, that the General had convinced a charity to donate. The children seemed as happy to see me as I was to see them. My husband and I stood for a while and watched them march south toward 18th Street.

When the children arrived at school the next Monday, they told me their band had been in a parade in the park. They talked about how the General took care of the children for the mothers and let the band practice in his house on the third floor.

Mary was a child with exceptionally dark skin. The others called her Black Girl. Ivory said, "Hey, Katie, yo is sittin' side a black girl. You got a black girl sittin' side a you."

Katie moved and said, "I ain't gonna sit side no black girl. Hey, black girl, move ovah."

Chapter Four

Mary hit at Katie, as she often did when someone called her Black Girl, and Katie hit back. When I got them settled down, I said, "You know, there are better ways of settling an argument than hitting. Mary could tell Katie she didn't like to be called Black Girl instead of hitting her. Katie could say she didn't like to be hit, instead of hitting back."

Katie said, "My mama told me to hit anybody who hit me."

Ivory said, "My mama said if anybody hit me, to slap him in the face."

I said, "Just play a game with Mary, just once. Don't hit her back and see what will happen."

Katie said, "I ain't never gonna let nobody hit me les' I hit um back. Dat's what my mama said."

This was not the only time I tried to get the kindergartners to try something besides hitting back. But my admonishments didn't work. The "hit back" attitude was too deeply ingrained.

Later that day I overheard Lisa saying a rhyme. My ears always opened when I heard a rhyme. "Black is beautiful, brown is neat, yellow is mellow, but white is. . ." Her hand went over her mouth when she saw me. "Oh, we can't tell *you*. . ." I thought she was going to say because I was white, but she said, "You might tell Mr. Breen."

I said, "Lisa, what we say in our classroom is just for us. I don't tell Mr. Breen what happens here."

She raised her eyebrows as she said, "I don't know no white people, just Mr. Breen."

I said, "Think about it, Lisa, don't you know any white person except Mr. Breen?"

Teachah Don't Know Nothin'

"No, just Mr. Breen."

I sat down in one of the small chairs nearby and called the children around me. "Lisa said she doesn't know any white people except Mr. Breen. Do any of you know any other white person?"

They looked at each other as though they were trying to help each other think, but concluded that they knew no white person except Mr. Breen.

"Mary, come here," I said. I put my hand and Mary's hand together, and asked, "Do you see any difference in the color?"

Lisa yelled, "Hey, yawl, look! We got a white teachah! We got a white teachah!" They all chanted together, "We got a white teachah!"

I let that chant continue until *they* stopped it. Their rhythmic words hugged me. I'd felt so much like an outsider and they were saying I belonged.

Chapter Five

I completed my year at Haven School and took a job in Oak Park as reading consultant for the fall. I had my own office, well stocked with all the newest and best reading materials. Children expected to learn and teachers expected them to learn. It was so much like the Palatine-Arlington Heights schools that I felt like I'd come home.

One day I was sitting in my office during lunch and heard loud gum popping on the stairs outside the door. As quick as a shotgun blast, the sound took me back to Haven School. I said aloud, "I don't belong here. I belong in Chicago."

It was in that instant that I realized how much I had enjoyed my time in Chicago, and knew without a doubt I wanted to go back to teaching in the inner city schools. I missed those children. In Oak Park, life was easy and

Teachah Don't Know Nothin'

predictable. I couldn't recall even one predictable day at Haven School. Yes, I missed Chicago's kids.

Two years passed before I was able to return, this time as a substitute teacher. Again I was assigned to Area B.

Forestville School was my first assignment, farther south than Haven. The old brick building was huge, three floors high. As I looked for a place to park, three boys - about ten years old - began running alongside the car. One jumped on the hood. I stopped the car quickly, wondering what to do. I wasn't afraid - for the boys were laughing and having fun. I rolled down the window, stuck my head out, and motioned for them to come to me. "Do you guys know where teachers are supposed to park?" They pointed to a fenced-in lot at the back of the building, and stood on the sidewalk as they watched me drive away.

Forestville was another antiquated building, this one with bars on windows on the lower floors. A guard sat at the top of each flight of stairs. My class was junior high math on the third floor, a dingy classroom, with torn shades over dirty windows, and glass broken from the doors covering the bookshelves on the back wall. The teacher had left textbooks and a lesson plan. As I looked at the teacher's edition my heart sank. New math! I didn't know the meaning of the words!

Thirty-five kids came in noisily. I had written the day's assignment on the board and gradually they got seated and began to talk quietly with each other. Nobody started working and nobody paid any attention to me. I chose a guy in the middle of a group and said to him, "Do you have paper?"

Chapter Five

"Yes."
"Do you have a pencil?"
"Yes."
"Do you have a book?"
"Yes."
"Do you know how to do the work?"
"Yes."
A girl near him said, "She wants you to get to work."
Another boy said, "She think we 'sposed to be quiet and not talk." They gradually began working and I relaxed.

Second period was science, in the lab. I lined the kids up and took them to the science lab only to find out there was no science when the science teacher was absent. The students knew that and were having a little fun at my expense. But what was I going to do with them for the next hour?

Well, animals might be considered good subjects for science. "OK, class, since we can't have science, I'll give you a special treat. I'll tell you about my adventures in the Canadian wilderness." I told them about hunters and fishermen, about bears, moose, deer and fish, and running a generator for electricity. I told them about taking the boat nine miles, hiking a mile uphill, and driving 38 miles of abandoned mining roads to get to town. The kids listened and asked questions and we had a great time.

At noon I wanted to make a telephone call and asked the principal where to find a phone. "It's in the teacher's lounge, but teachers don't use it much." She walked with me to the basement and unlocked the door. "Check

Teachah Don't Know Nothin'

carefully to see that the door is locked when you leave and don't let anyone in."

While we were still standing there with the door open, another substitute came in with a cola in her hand. The principal said to her, "You know, no food or drinks are allowed above the basement level." I smiled but didn't say anything. Her words were funny because the students ate in the classroom constantly, and the floors were littered with candy wrappers and sunflower seed shells. As I left I noticed iron-bar security doors, pushed open, at doorways to the lunchroom and gym. I wondered why those rooms needed that kind of security.

After lunch, one of the boys came in swinging a chain two or three feet long that had 12-inch wooden pieces about the width of a broom handle on each end of the chain. I'd never seen such a thing and said, "Oh, come here. Let me see your chain."

He looked at me with his eyes wide, put the chain down to his side, and looked around at the others as if they would tell him what to do. He looked uncomfortable so I said, "I'll tell you what, put it in your desk until the end of the period, then you can demonstrate how you use it." I thought it was some kind of baton, something used for tricks or athletic games. Near the end of the period I said, "Come, show the class how to use your sticks."

He shook his head and said, "Oh, no, that's OK." He pushed the sticks farther into his desk. I was disappointed, but he absolutely refused to perform. As he left the room he held his sticks close by his side and away from me, as if he didn't want me to see them.

Chapter Five

Next period a boy leaned out the window, yelled to someone on the sidewalk below, and threw wadded up papers out. When he refused to get to his seat, I wrote a pass and sent him to the office.

When I tried to check attendance the kids wouldn't tell me their names. I asked a boy near the front if he would help me check attendance and the kids threatened to get him if he did. The boy who seemed to be the biggest troublemaker sat in a back seat. When I went back and tried to talk to him, he made under-the-breath threats that I ignored. I went back to the front of the room.

These kids weren't going to cooperate, that was plain. What could I do to get their attention? I felt frustrated and very irritated with myself because I couldn't figure out any strategy that would get them orderly.

Since I didn't know modern math I put some simple multiplication problems on the board. Those problems seemed too difficult, so I put up some one-digit problems from the multiplication tables. Evidently they were more comfortable with that arithmetic, and soon they were quiet and working. These students weren't any more ready for modern math than I was.

As I locked the door and walked to the office I was thinking that my first day as a substitute teacher had been a colossal failure. When the principal asked if I would be able to return the next day, I hesitated a moment, then asked, "Same room?" When she said no, I agreed to return.

From school I went to visit a friend who lived on the south side. When I told her where I'd been she said, "My dear, didn't anyone warn you? That's the worst school in the

Teachah Don't Know Nothin'

city. It's an area where Caucasians are not welcome. You don't know what danger you were in. I'm black, and there are areas of Chicago not safe for me, and that's one of them. Don't go back there."

I told her about the kid who had the sticks on the chain. "That's a lethal weapon and dangerous. You should have reported him." No wonder he wouldn't demonstrate how he used it.

Though the principal had promised another room, next morning the secretary directed me to the same one. The morning went fairly smoothly with the simple multiplication problems I'd put on the board. During lunch I was sitting at the desk grading papers, no one else in the room, when a tall, heavy-set, scary-looking black boy walked in carrying a stick.

"You remember yesterday, don't ya?" he asked in a threatening low voice. I pulled myself lower to the papers I was grading at the desk and thought, oh, dear, now I'm in for it.

"No," I said. "What happened yesterday?"

"You know what you done to my cousin?"

"No, I don't know what happened to your cousin. Who is your cousin? "

"My cousin! You got my cousin in trouble yesterday."

"I don't remember getting anybody in trouble." I kept my head down and tried to become part of the desk as he came closer to my back.

He yelled, "My cousin, you sent him to the principal! You got him in trouble!"

Chapter Five

"I don't know your cousin. Are you sure I'm the teacher you're looking for?"

"Oh, forget it! I'll let you off this time." It was as though I had to be aware of why he was angry or he couldn't do anything to me.

As he was walking toward the door, I said, "Hey, come back here." He stopped. "Your cousin's a real stinker, you know."

"Yeah, but what did he do to you?"

"He didn't do anything to me, but he sure played havoc in my classroom. Now, tell me what I can do to get him to behave himself."

"Here." He held his stick out to me.

"Oh, no," I said, "I could never hit anybody."

"Ain't no other way. You just have to whup him with somethin'. Now, write me a pass. I'm late to class."

I wrote the pass. He looked it over. "This ain't no good. You didn't do it right. Make me another one." I did, with his help. As he was walking out the door, he said, "I can't get in no more trouble. If I do they gonna send me to Montefiore."

"Montefiore? What's that?"

"Don't you know nothin'? That's the school where they send all the bad kids."

"Why would they send *you* there?"

"I don't know," he said as he was leaving. "The teachers here just don't like me. Don't none o' the teachers like me. Better get goin' now or I'll be in trouble again."

I was standing at the window when the kids came in after lunch, and some of them came over to stand beside me.

Teachah Don't Know Nothin'

One of them said, "Oh, he gonna git her." A woman was walking on the sidewalk on the opposite side of the street with a man walking about half a block behind her.

I couldn't see anything strange in the situation. "How do you know he's going to get her?"

They looked at me as if I was stupid, and someone said, "You can see it in his eyes." We could not see his eyes from our third floor window.

The woman turned, coming back in our direction. When she didn't continue the way she was going I thought she was safe. The man followed. She walked to a semi-truck cab standing outside the school and talked to the driver.

One of the kids said, "He ain't gonna do nothin." And he didn't. She walked another direction with the man still following her.

"Why doesn't she come in the school for help?"

"You crazy, lady?"

"What's he going to do to her?

"Oh, rob her, or kill her." The even tone of voice made either alternative seem equal in importance.

I said, "But how can he rob her? She doesn't have a purse."

"Yo sho is dumb, lady. She keep it in her titties and he jist go down in dare and git it."

The woman changed directions.

"Why is she going that way?"

"He making her go dat way so his partner can git her."

The man and woman walked out of our sight, and we got to work. Since I hadn't changed the math problems I'd put

Chapter Five

on the board the day before, I decided to let them write about what they wanted for their future.
One girl wrote:
>This book is about me and Mrs. Oglesby. I want to be a teacher and before I be a teacher I want to be a housewife and I going to school to be a teacher. I like to dance and I like to sing. I like to skates. I like to were pants and dress. I like you Mrs. Oglesby. You is a very nice lady. You do not shout out and you talk so nice. I like you very, very much. I wish you was our division teacher and our math teacher too. The end for Jessica Newton.

I was pleased to know at least one student liked me, but I did not return the next day.

Chapter Six

The first day at Douglass, I was assigned to a class of sixth graders. It was a class of BD kids - behavior disordered. Though there were only a dozen students, I found it almost impossible to get their attention and get them quiet. A big boy with mischievous-looking eyes sat grinning at me and hitting his pencil on a desk as hard and loud as he could. I walked back to him and said, "Do you know any tunes you can drum with your pencil?" That did it. The kids drummed on their desks and books and soon were singing songs and rhymes along with their drumming. No schoolwork, but they were no longer running around and yelling.

A girl with short braids that stuck up on her head like spikes, who did not participate in the singing and drumming, came to me and whispered, "When that clock hangs on twelve, we go to eat."

Teachah Don't Know Nothin'

I tried to line the students up in the room for the walk to the lunchroom. As I was standing at the door with my hand on the doorknob, the pencil-drumming boy pushed by me and climbed through the opening in the door where a glass window used to be. Others followed. I opened the door and let them all go. They ran to the lunchroom. I followed, almost at a run.

When the principal asked how the morning had gone, I told her it wasn't too bad until time to line up for lunch and then I lost them. She said, "Well, if you lasted that long you've done well. Most substitutes don't last an hour in that room."

For the first period after lunch I had hall guard duty. This meant I sat in a chair, or stood, and kept an eye on things. The chair was near a noisy classroom. I said to one of the boys who came outside, "Aren't you supposed to be in class?"

"Yes," he answered.

"Why are students in the hall, and why is so much noise going on in the class?"

He said, "She afraid to hit 'em. Dey do anything dey want to."

"Is it the regular teacher, or a substitute?"

"Da regular teacher."

I was curious. "Is she black or white?"

"White."

Later, while in the washroom, I was humming and singing softly when a teacher came in. She said, "You can tell you haven't been around here long. Nobody sings here."

Chapter Six

As we talked I figured out that she was the teacher who was "afraid to hit 'em." She asked if I'd had any trouble with the kids since *Roots* had shown on TV. She said, "The kids all think I did it to them. They even get down and laugh and make fun of me and say, 'Yes, Massa, Toby be a good slave.'"

Two weeks had passed since the TV movie. I'd heard a lot of comments by the children. They made remarks that made it clear that they thought what happened in the movie was happening today instead of years ago. One kid said, "You know what yo grandfathah did to my grandfathah, don't you?" I explained that I didn't know about any of the things my grandfather did, but I wished the awful things hadn't happened to their grandfathers.

In an eighth-grade class later in the day, I asked a girl to pick up some papers she had thrown on the floor. In a teasing, high-pitched voice she stood, twisted her body, and said, "Yes, Massa, Toby pick up da papers. Toby be a good slave!" She looked so funny that I started laughing and couldn't stop. The class looked shocked and became so quiet that even after I could stop, I kept laughing awhile, then, wiped my eyes. The students turned their attention back to their assignment and caused no problems for the remainder of the period.

At the end of the day, as I was leaving the room, I picked up a paper from the floor. The paper was carefully folded. It was a note that said: "Bernice, if Kim had a gun up to your head and told you to suck his dick or will you rather get shot in the head. He say he will shot you if you don't.

Teachah Don't Know Nothin'

what will you do tell the truth." The note was written in pencil, the answer in ink: "Get shot."

I was on hall duty the next day when three boys came racing down the hall chased by a girl. She was about ten or eleven, with her hair pushed back in an unkempt way as though it had been fixed hastily, and her socks drooped down over the tops of her shoes. I grabbed her, pulled her to me.

She spurted, "Them boys always teasin' me cause I got problems and make trouble. I make trouble 'cause Mr. Jordan calls me a 'little terror' and gets mad at me when the other kids do bad things."

I said, "Where's your room?" She didn't seem to hear me, just kept talking.

"I live with my mothah. Ain't got no fathah. My real fathah is old. I talked to him on the phone once. He rich. My auntie tried to take me away from my mothah. They had a fight but I have to stay with my mothah. I have to help her with da work. She ain't got nobody else."

She had huge dark eyes, a wide mouth with thick lips, and a protruding chin. Her turtleneck sweater hugged her neck. She kept talking. "The man who used to stay with her she didn't marry but he went to jail, one jail and another kind of jail. I'm glad 'cause he had a gun. My gran'mothah not really my gran'mothah. She gran'mothah for everybody, she think my mothah don't work, but she do, two jobs, Avon and anothah job."

Without a pause, she continued. "Black people don't live too long. I don't got no friends. My best friend is my cousin but she don't go to this school. Last night my cousin got

Chapter Six

mad in the elevator and took out her knife and started cutting people. She was on da way to her house on 14. One boy was bleeding 'cause he got cut, and a little boy got his finger cut off."

I liked hall duty because it gave me a chance to talk to the children individually, but I didn't often meet anybody this talkative. I asked her, "Did the police come?"

"Yeah, dey come."

"What did they do to her?"

"Dey didn't find her."

"What about the hurt people?"

"Dey took dem to the doctah."

I changed the subject. "Are you the only one who gets in trouble in your class?"

"Sidney out walking in da hall and he in trouble. You know him, he ugly. He got a round head dat stick out in front."

About that time a boy walked by and she said, "Dat Sidney." I didn't see anything ugly about him, but his head did have an odd shape.

"I act bad 'cause the teacher tells me I'm a terror. The ladies in da office said I'm a terror. I get mad and run out of Mr. Jordan's room 'cause I don't like him.'

I said, "I think it's time for you to go back to your class now."

As she walked away, from down the hall in the other direction I heard a girl's voice saying, "I'm gonna kick yo ...!" I looked at the girl as she looked at me. Her angry-looking face flashed me a big grin, then switched back to the angry look. In a lower voice she swore and frowned,

Teachah Don't Know Nothin'

again flashed me a big grin, then turned and continued her swearing.

I laughed to myself. How funny to see her switch her facial gestures so quickly. I wished I had a movie camera to catch her quick changes. She paid no more attention to me, so maybe she didn't notice when I laughed.

After only a few days at Douglass School, I was sent to Oakland School. Usually Sub Center called each morning at seven to tell me which school I'd be working at that day. After a few days at Oakland, I was asked to be the 8:30 Sub, which meant I would be there everyday, and fill in wherever needed.

While at Oakland, I discovered how much the children enjoyed learning to write and read rhymes. In a grade-four class I gave the children booklets of lined paper with construction paper covers, and put rhymes on the board for them to copy, rhymes they knew and a few they didn't know. One girl picked up the booklet that contained my collected rhymes and wanted to copy it. She said, "This is Black." She smiled as she held onto the booklet, "You got some in here I don't know." I think she copied them all. Different communities had different rhymes, and often the same rhymes had some words that were different.

When class was over the children were still writing and didn't want to leave. The principal came by to see how things were going. He said, "I knew you wouldn't have any trouble." I was shocked when anyone made such a comment. Although I was becoming more confident about my abilities, I was still uncertain about how I would manage with each new group. I always had to be alert to

Chapter Six

what would work here, what would work there. I was finding that substituting, and continually facing different situations, helped me develop stronger teaching skills.

I followed the lesson plan the teacher left if at all possible. Sometimes I came up with my own plan. I carried a bag with colored markers, pictures of Canada (to use when telling my adventure stories), and other miscellaneous items. Many times teachers didn't leave lesson plans. Many times the lesson plan didn't work. Many times the kids finished the lesson early. Then what would I do? I tried to be prepared, so that whatever came up I would be able to manage.

Chapter Seven

In an EMH class (Educable Mentally Handicapped) with kids 12 to 15 years old, I put rhymes on the board. The room was so quiet all morning that the principal was curious. Every time I looked out the door he was standing there. At noon he looked at me and smiled a big smile and made the V-for-victory sign.

In the afternoon, one of the younger boys that the other kids said "always acted crazy" took his turn at the board, using the pointer stick to read the rhymes. He kept reading the jump rope rhyme called "Winstons" so he could get to the last line.

> Winstons taste good like a cigarette should,
> Winstons taste good like a cigarette should,
> Uh, ah, I want a piece of pie.
> The pie's too sweet,
> I want a piece of meat.

Teachah Don't Know Nothin'

    The meat's too tough,
      I want to make love.
He whistled and drew a circle around the last line. "I like that," he said. "Our teacher don't do no things like poems for us, she just makes us read."

I told him that's what he'd been doing, reading.

He said, "Dat ain't no readin', dat's poems," and kept on reading with the pointer stick.

They copied the poems into a booklet, and as they worked they were aware that the room was more quiet than usual. One of the girls said, "Eugene most of the time acts crazy."

Another said, "Willie most of the time chases Anna around the room."

A little later someone else said, "Most of the time the boys gets into fights."

Nearly all the boys had learned the four poems before the day was over and wanted more. The one girl in the group had trouble copying from the board so one of the boys made her booklet.

When school was over the principal told me that particular class was always a problem. When the teacher was away and a substitute had to be called in, the students usually raced all over the school. Thank goodness I had discovered how much the kids, younger and older, liked writing and reading rhymes.

Sometimes, with the younger children, one poem or song was enough for the day. They'd copy it, and take turns reading or singing it with the pointer stick, then illustrate it.

Chapter Seven

One song that worked exceptionally well with younger children was "A Big Black Dog."

A big black dog sat on the back porch
And Bingo was his name.
B-I-N-G-O, B-I-N-G-O, B-I-N-G-O,
And Bingo was his name, O.

By the end of the day they could read it from the board and had their copies to take home so they could read it to their parents.

In a fifth-grade classroom I told the children about a problem I had. My daughter was coming home from boarding school, and would be going to a public school. Since our apartment complex was in Area B, near Michael Reese Hospital on the south side, she would be required to attend Phillips High School, where the Haven kids with sixth-grade or below reading levels were sent.

I had mentioned the situation to the principal earlier and he said he knew of only one thing to do and it wasn't legal: Use a false address.

A teacher-aide at breakfast said, "They'll kill her." The response from the children was the same.

"Dey'll kill 'er!"

"She bettah not go in the washroom. Girls git stabbed in dare. They stabbed a pregnant girl in da stomach."

"Da boys'll like her; dey won't hurt her. Da girls be mad."

I pulled Samantha's picture from my wallet and passed it around. One of the girls came up with a solution. "She got black hair and black eyes, maybe she could pass for light, not white." She hesitated, and asked, "But do she talk like you?"

Teachah Don't Know Nothin'

"Yes, she talks the way I do."

"Den she can't pass."

The kids had such strong feelings and opinions about Samantha going to Phillips that I asked them if they'd like to write her a letter and tell her what they thought. They liked the idea. From about twenty letters, here are excerpts:

> Phillips is a nice school, but it not fit for a nice girl like you. They will not except you for who you are but of your color.

> Do not go to Phillips as they might beat you up. I no that you are white and if you go to Phillips the children will not like you. You are to pretty to get kill.

> You should not go to the black school because they hate white people. I know. I am black. But I like white people. You should try to go to white people school.

> My cousin got stab on the chin. I just know one thing about Phillips, it is danger. They kill around there too much and its strange things going on, so please tell your mother that you rather go some where else than Phillips. And the reason why I know is because I stay around there. You wouldn't won't to get killed would you?

> I like to give you some advice. Don't you know that around about three people got killed in that school? One girl and two boys got killed in the girls and boys washroom and I wouldn't want you to get hurt. Please be careful.

The next morning in the lunchroom during breakfast one of the girls drew me aside and said, "Mrs. Ogleby, please

Chapter Seven

don't let your daughter go to Phillips. You know how black peoples is. Dey don't like white people, and she'll get hurt."

Samantha knew there was no way we would let her go to Phillips, but I did share the letters with her. She loved reading them. The end of the story was that we moved to the suburbs.

Soon after this, I was sent to cover a fourth-grade classroom where the kids were noisy. The teacher yelled, telling them to get in their seats, threatening to send them to the office if they couldn't behave. She waved her 18-inch ruler wrapped thick with masking tape that seemed to be standard equipment in most classrooms. I knew this would be a hard group.

The kids were still noisy when she left. On her desk she had left some papers for me to correct, and some reading worksheets to pass out.

Calling such a noisy group to order almost never worked. I usually tried to target the noisiest child and start talking quietly to him, or her - usually a boy but not always. My plan wasn't working. The class was still noisy. As I walked around, I caught part of a conversation between some boys.

"She afraid."

"She ain't afraid."

"She white, and she afraid."

"She ain't afraid."

I went back to the desk and bided my time while I corrected papers. I was staying out of the way and trying to give the students a chance to come to order on their own when I overheard a boy saying a rhyme about Charlie

Teachah Don't Know Nothin'

Chan. I called him to me and told him I collected rhymes and would like to get that one written down. He hesitated.

His name was Tommy, a light-skinned boy in an orangey-red shirt. He didn't want to say the rhyme. He said Anthony told it to him, so I sent him to get Anthony. Neither boy would say the rhyme. Anthony put his hand over his mouth and spoke through his fingers: "It's a dirty song."

That was the first time I'd heard a child call any of the rhymes dirty, so I was especially curious. I told the boys I was saving all kinds of poems, and with a little more coaxing, they said the rhyme while I wrote it down.

> Charlie Chan was a great old man,
> He walked down the street with his dick in his hand.
> He done it, and done it, and done it,
> Until his dick got sore.
> He went upstairs and done it some more.
> He went to the doctor and the doctor said,
> "Sorry, Charlie, but yo dick is dead."
> He said, "Doctor, doctor, it can't be true!"
> "Sorry, Charlie, but yo balls is too."

One of them immediately started on George Washington, and the other joined in.

> George Washington was a great old man,
> He jumped out the window with his dick in his hand.
> He said, "Pardon me, ma'am,
> I'm just doin' my duty.
> Drop your drawers and I'll fuck you in the booty."

Chapter Seven

I couldn't believe I was sitting there writing those words in a classroom, or anywhere, for that matter. The boys were not embarrassed. I was.

Another boy had a big grin on his face while showing a magazine called Jungle Jim Screw to the others. A prissy little girl said, "That stuff don't even excite me. I just looks at it and trip out."

A boy retorted, "Jist cause you don't git none!"

"I gits it when I wants it," she said with a shrug of her shoulders.

"When he give it to you, you mean."

She lifted the sides of her skirt and twirled around, saying, "When I wants it I takes it!" She strutted over to a girl nearby and said, "I make my pimp pimp yo pimp."

When one of the boys ran to the door, I looked up. He said in a matter of fact way, "I thought it was my lady peeping in the door."

These were little kids. I wondered if they really were having sex or just talking about it, or if they even knew what the words meant.

I should have known seatwork wasn't the thing for this group. I passed out the reading worksheets. Within minutes I realized the work was too difficult. They didn't understand what to do, and giving directions to twenty of them at once wasn't an option. As I was helping Albert, James, who had been a little demon all afternoon, sneaked to the back of the group, grabbed at Melissa, and ran back to his seat. Melissa screamed and began crying. James had yanked her earring from her ear. The earring broke, and the ripped ear was bleeding.

Teachah Don't Know Nothin'

As Melissa cried, she dropped her purse on the floor and its contents spilled out. James grabbed her dollar, and Albert got her quarter.

I went for the dollar and got it away from James. He held up his fist and yelled, "I'll git you, teachah. When ya finds something, ya keeps it. If ya lose it, ya loses it!" Albert, with the quarter, dashed out of the room. I didn't follow him. It was more important to quiet the class.

We began to talk about what Albert had done. For the first time, the students were orderly and speaking one at a time. They suggested things to be done to Albert such as black his eyes, beat him with the ruler, and hit him with a ball bat.

Melissa sat looking away from the group, holding a tissue to her ear. I asked her to tell us what she thought, but she wouldn't talk.

In that same school I had an interesting conversation with a seven-year-old.

That day I was tutoring students in a vacant room. As soon as she came in the room she put her hands behind her back and stuck her chin out. "My name is Sandra," she said with a shake of her pigtails. "I stays at 1420 State Street, on the 16 flo."

I said, "Oh, I heard a man fell out of one of the buildings on State Street. Was that your building?"

"A man fell out 1520, dat's not my building." She sat down beside me, straightened her skirt, then said, "A man came in at night time and tried to kill my mothah. And

Chapter Seven

what happened was, they got my auntie. She got kilt. And I has to shot 'im. My mama, she played like she was asleep."

Her voice dropped to a soft, slow whisper. "And den, I picked up the gun, *real* quiet, and my mama picked up the knife, *real* quiet."

"What happened when you picked up the gun?"

"First I shot 'im, and den my mama stabbed him and throwed him out the 16 windah."

"What happened to him?"

"He died."

"He died?"

"Cose he died. I shot 'im and my mama stabbed 'im. He couldn't come back to life. Dey didn't put no ice pack on 'im and he couldn't come back to life."

I tried to get her to pay attention to the pictures in the workbook. She said, "Uh-huh," and kept talking. After several more of my attempts to interest her in the workbook, she said, "Now, I can only do one page, 'cause my mama said to only do one pages cause my head'll be hurtin' if I do mo' than one pages, den I have to go back to the hospital."

"Were you in the hospital?"

"Yeah, ever time I go."

"Why do you go to the hospital?"

"'Cause I got kidneys. And they have to give me a shot. When I get the shot, I don't be scared. I don't even cry. I don't never cry."

"Did you ever have an operation?"

"I had a operation 'cause I have to go to the hospital for my ear, 'cause sometimes it hurt in my ear."

Teachah Don't Know Nothin'

"We only have a few words to read," I said. We read mat, man, and added map, and drew lines to the pictures.

She closed the workbook and asked, "Do you have a boyfriend? Don't all girls s'posed to have a boyfriend? I have one. My sistah, she told me to get one boyfriend. She say take one at a time in boyfriends. When the one boy quit me and go with another girl, then the next day I have me another boyfriend. When he quit me den I go with another boy. "

I opened the book and pointed to cat and can, but I was thinking that she was a cute little girl and could get boyfriends when she wanted them. Here she was at seven years of age planning her romances.

When I substituted in one of the eighth-grade classes the teacher left a note for me at the end of her lesson plan. "Good luck! Don't expect much of these kids. They're very dumb."

I looked over the assignments she had left and knew they were too difficult. I decided to write one of my own on the board: Copy these rhymes. Then write other rhymes you know.

During the next hour the students worked diligently. Once again I saw that if the students had work to do that interested them and that they could do, they were well behaved.

Chapter Eight

Another day when I worked with individual children who either needed help reading or were discipline problems. I met Andy, a chubby boy whose shirt buttons strained around his middle. He had been causing problems in his class. He began talking right away about the ghosts in his house. "I don't know what they made out of."

I said, "Well, maybe they're not made out of anything. Other people probably can't see them, just you."

"You know them shadows real. Them shadows on the wall."

I decided to say something that might help him not be afraid. "Next time you're alone in your room, all by yourself, you could think of a name for your ghost. And after you get a name, you could think of him as a friendly ghost who takes care of you. Get yourself a good ghost that

Teachah Don't Know Nothin'

will stay with you and keep anything bad from happening to you."

He rubbed a hand across his very short black hair and smiled at me. "You so glad you got you a ghost, huh?"

"Oh, yes. I have a friendly ghost."

"And don't yo house look full o' roaches?"

I didn't understand what he said. "What?"

"Don't yo house look full o' roaches?"

"Well, not very many roaches."

"But don't yo house look good? How yo house look?"

"I'll show you a picture of it." I was living at Lake Point Tower at that time and had a postcard picture of the building. "I live on the 42nd floor," I said, pointing to about where the 42nd floor would be.

He said, "My mama go right around dare." He looked some more. "It look scary. It might burn down. I'll show you a picture of mine. Mine is red and white. Close your eyes."

I did, and he drew a picture of a big building. "Dat's my house," he said. "Now, I'm gonna draw a picture of me and I'm gonna draw you. I'm a artist, didn't nobody tell you that? I don't know why these ghostes and these monsters keep botherin' me. They don't bother nobody else. I'm gonna make a picture of a ghost. I'm bad with that drawin' stuff."

After I admired his artwork, he asked, " What if I act bad? If I act bad my ghost gonna git me?"

"Your own ghost likes you all the time, if you're good or bad. If you act really bad, he'll help you act good."

"If somebody beat me up, will he help me fight back?"

Chapter Eight

"He might see you don't get hurt too much."

"I got a little ghost. The curtains come open and closed back up and the ghost come out of it." He looked at me and grinned, his eyes sparkling, and said, "You gonna fake me. You ain't got no ghost."

"Oh, yes, I have good ghosts that stay around me all the time, " I said. "And you are a good artist."

"Now I'm gonna draw a big circle, and put my ghosts in it. Now, you talk to them and tell them to go away."

Larry came running in, a short skinny little boy. His pants and shirt were way too big. I thought Andy ought to swap clothes with him. Andy told Larry about his ghosts, and Larry said, "Ghosts don't s'posed to help nobody."

I said, "Andy's ghost is his friend, and is helping him. Now, let's get to our reading."

This wasn't the only time I heard students talk about ghosts. A favorite subject, they were. One story came from Freddie, a third grade boy who was light-skinned and had longer, bushier hair than the other boys. While the other children were working in their workbooks, he told me the following story about his grandmother:

"My gran'mama come back. She fell down de stairs, and hit her head. They operated on 'er, but she died. I went to the funeral and den went to a movie, and came home about ten a'clock. She come, an' my gran'daddy turn on de lights and he tell her to git out."

"Why did he turn on the light?" I asked.

" 'Cause you can't see 'er when the lights on. You see 'er when you cut off de lights, or dey cut themse'f off."

"And what do you do when she comes?"

Teachah Don't Know Nothin'

"The TV be still on when you go to sleep at ten. And den, boy I be scared. She come to my gran'daddy room first, den she come in my room. She stay dare 'bout - long time. I be looking at da cuckoo clock. I snuck out a da bed 'cause I knowed she was fixin' to come."

"Dey shaved my gran'mama's hair. Dey have to cut it 'cause her hair was long, and den dey put a wig on her head. Dey gave da hair to my gran'daddy. He be skeered to death. My lil' cousin was playin' and tried to hit me wid it, but it didn't hit me. It hit my gran'daddy. Den he got holt o' my lil' cousin. He got a hose pipe line out da room, and he whupped him all da way out de house downstairs to my auntie's house wid dat hose pipe. I couldn't git out my doh cause my gran'mama was dare, and couldn't get the window open, cause she was dare."

One of the children sitting nearby asked, "How do yo gran'mama get in?"

Freddie said, "Sometime she fly. My lil' cousin named Punkin, she pushed de windah shut. My gran'mama carry you off, you know, havin' her arms like dis." He held his arms out in front of him, palms up.

Yolanda jumped in with her story. Her voice was husky and deep, with the tone storytellers take on to tell ghost stories. She said, "It was late and my mothah had came back alive. I heard my mothah knockin' on the back doh, and I be ske-e-ered. Den when I go to sleep, den my mothah come in. Den ever'body be seein' her, and when dey see her dey scream. Den dey run in de washroom."

Like the children in other Chicago inner city classrooms, the ones in this third grade liked to talk about ghosts and

Chapter Eight

tell about seeing them. I was impressed with how serious they were during these discussions. There was no joking around when they talked about dead people who came back to visit.

Chapter Nine

Whenever I went to a new school, I judged whether it would be an easy or difficult day's work by the appearance of the school and neighborhood. Judging by what I could see, Suder School on West Washington Boulevard would be a good one. While the store fronts a few blocks away had bars on the doors and windows - some of them with pull-down solid steel barriers over their fronts - there were not many businesses in the area, just lots of high-rise apartments, Chicago housing project buildings, and the Chicago Stadium. No police or guards in sight. Maybe I would like to stay in this school for a while.

I was assigned to the Intermediate EMH (Educable Mentally Handicapped) classroom on the second floor. On the blackboard were some leftover easy assignments, so I changed the spelling words and the numbers in the

Teachah Don't Know Nothin'

arithmetic problems. Since I had arrived early, I had time to get well prepared. I made two nametags for each student: one for the child and one for the desk. Only eleven names were listed in the attendance book.

I was standing outside the door as the children, fourth- and fifth-graders, made their way up the stairs. They appeared sluggish - leaning against the rail and pulling themselves up. They paid little attention to me as they slouched into the room and began talking with each other, standing at the windows, sitting on desks, and walking about. Their clothes looked like they'd slept in them. Most of them frowned and looked angry. I wondered whether they were angry because I was there, because they had to come to school, or because of something that had happened at home.

They paid no attention to my directions to sit down so the day's work could start. I went to the boy who seemed most active and asked him to help me check attendance, which he did.

Whenever I tried to say something to the group, one of the kids would swear at me and then pretend I wasn't there. I watched them carefully, trying to figure out how to proceed. After about half an hour, one of them started to work on the assignments, and gradually they all began working, but never all at the same time. At least one or two were at their desks writing at any given time during the morning.

Recess time brought major revolution. They hid behind desks and doors, and ran the other way when I called. "I ain't going outside. Get the hell out of here. I ain't going

Chapter Nine

outside, you old white-assed lady. I grabbed the most rambunctious, Willie, who seemed to be the leader, and walked out with him. The others followed.

After recess, a band-aid I had on a finger came off and the cut began to bleed. Willie came over to look at it. He had a narrow face with huge eyes and long lashes, and very dark skin. He got a paper towel, wet it at the sink in the room, and wrapped it around my finger. I let him go to the office to see if there were any band-aids. He came back with a big grin on his face and a band-aid. He gently set to work to fix the new band-aid on my finger just right. It didn't seem possible that this was the same child who only a few minutes before had been swearing and calling me "white honky bitch."

While Willie worked with the band-aid, Joyce ran around the room hitting at people and taking things from the other kids. Willie said to her, "Shut up and sit down, black bitch, or I'm gonna get up and knock the shit outta your ass."

Joyce looked cute, with her tousled hair pulled back with a red hair band, but her actions and words were not cute. She calmed down and came over to me. "You got any kids?"

"Yes, I have children."

"Is they white-skinned like you?"

"Yes," I said.

"Is dey any black people in yo family?"

"I don't have any black people in my family as far as I know. Do you have any white people in your family?"

She jerked her head up, her eyes got big, and she walked away.

Teachah Don't Know Nothin'

The children continued to sporadically sit at their desks and write a little between talking and walking around the room. Afternoon was a different matter. "We don't work after lunch," they informed me, and began to throw erasers at the wastebaskets and an empty aquarium. The girls got out their jump rope.

The students in this class had I.Q. scores ranging from 62 to 79, but after I'd worked with them a few days I figured the low scores related to their environment, not innate ability.

Once when I suggested to one of the girls that she get to work, her eyes flashed at me. She looked at the sign on the door and said, "Don't matter no how. We ain't never gonna git out o' this MEH room." I didn't refute her words, for I thought she was right. Once labeled, the label would follow them.

I never knew what to expect from these fourth- and fifth-graders. One day they were relatively quiet and worked on their assignments, and I would feel that maybe a little progress had been made. The next day would be so hectic I despaired of anything valuable happening in that classroom. Within ten minutes of the opening of school one day, Eric was throwing books, Tyrone and Joyce were in a fight, Joyce got in a fight with Michael, Joyce hit Eric, and Michael took Joyce's hat and ran and fought with her. Joyce got mad and ran from the room. Cynthia picked up a deck of Old Maid cards and threw them all around the room.

Eric took things from the teacher's desk, and when I told him to put them back, he said, "Shut up fo I smack you." Then he wrote with a magic marker on a library book.

Chapter Nine

Willie said, "I ain't gonna do none of dat baby work!" Joyce was banging on the door to get in and Ruby wanted to let her in, but I told her to leave Joyce out there. Eric, from the back of the room, threw a book at the wastebasket. Cynthia opened the door for Joyce and ran out and down the hall yelling. Michael sat on the radiator kicking to make noise. Ruby stood at the door turning lights off and on until Willie ran up and hit her and made her cry. Eric took my shoes from under the desk and put them on.

I sat there wondering, what next? And whatever it was, how could I deal with it? Then I lost my cool. I picked up the ruler and banged it on the desk and yelled, "Now, sit down!"

Willy said, "Oh, shut up, bitch!" - then sat down.

Iris said, "You red-assed hoe bitch!" - then sat down.

Cynthia wrote a note and laid it on the desk in front of me, and sat down. The note said, "Miss Dee is a hoe." Soon the class was quiet. I felt awful. Never before had I yelled at the kids in any school, but at the same time I almost held my breath with the hope that the orderliness would last.

I let Willie pass out papers. When he was finished, he began putting back the pictures he had yanked off the bulletin board the day before when he got angry because I wouldn't let him pass out papers. While he was putting the pictures up he yelled, "Hey teachah, who is dese people?"

"They're famous people, Willie. They are black people and people who helped black people."

He snapped back quickly, "Oh, no. Nixon's on yo side."

He looked at a picture of Sammy Davis, Jr., and said, "Dat niggah! He think he white, but he a niggah!" I had

Teachah Don't Know Nothin'

learned that the children used the word nigger both as an insult and with affection. Sometimes neither -- just to talk about someone they knew. But heaven forbid that any white person should use the word.

Ruby, so tiny I didn't expect her to be feisty, wanted to help Willie with the board. When he wouldn't let her, she said, "You sucks yo mothah's pussy!"

He yelled back, "You sucks yo fathah's cock!"

The name-calling went on until I thought they had said about every hostile thing that could be thought of when Ruby said, under her breath so quietly I almost didn't hear her, "Yo mama..."

Willie jumped down from the chair he was standing on to put up the pictures, picked up the chair and started for Ruby. I was close enough to get between them before he reached her. "What's wrong, Willie? What did she do?"

"She said my mama. Ain't nobody gonna say my mama!" He ran around me and slapped Ruby, then went back to his bulletin board. I didn't understand, but I knew that whenever all the worst things had been done and said, all that was needed to get a good fight going was to say, "Yo mama."

After he was finished with the board, papers sticking out over the edges, Willie stood back, looked at his work and said, "Oh, teachah, don't dat look pretty?"

At lunch he said, "Teachah, when we git back to the room, I want you to help me with some spelling." This was certainly a new twist. He had never been eager to write before. As soon as we got back to the room he and Cynthia started to work. He asked, "How you spell 'very'?" Then, "

Chapter Nine

How you spell 'answer'?" When he was finished, he brought the note for me to check to see if he'd spelled all the words correctly.

The note read, Dear Debra, I like you very much. Do you like me? Send the answer back yes or no. Willie.

He asked permission to go to the washroom. When he was happy his eyes danced, and this time he was happy with all of his body and soul. I knew he wasn't really headed for the washroom.

I noticed that when I passed out candy to the children for a treat, each child gave a portion to Willie. I watched carefully, and sure enough, if there were two pieces, one went to Willie. Next time I made sure all the kids were at their desks and told them they weren't to get up until they'd eaten the candy. Then I saw them passing candy back to Willie. I was never able to stop the practice. They'd hide their treat from me and sneak part of it to Willie. Was it some kind of extortion? They seemed too young for that, but Willie's dominant personality could have pulled off such a thing. I never learned the answer to my question. I didn't ask, as I would do in other schools in years to come.

They were talking about Jew Town one day and when I said I didn't know what that was Cynthia wrote on the board, "Goo Twon." It was next door to "Shoe Twon." Best of all they liked to go to "Go Blacks," (Goldblatts) which had three doors and a telephone. Willie drew a map of how to take the bus down Madison Street to Maxwell Street. His picture of "Go Blacks" included the telephone. He explained that at Jew Town you could buy 5 pairs of socks "like dese" for $2.00, and 10 tapes for $2.00. You could

85

Teachah Don't Know Nothin'

take the bus down Madison, he said, at 7 o'clock, or 8 or 9 or anytime. "But don't eat the food," he said. "It ain't clean. De people cook and pick da noses at the same time."

One afternoon I played Old Maid cards with Ruby and the kids gathered around to watch. I said, "Do I draw from you?"

'No, you pulls from me," she said. She jutted out her chin and looked me in the eye.

"Oh, I see," I said. "I draw cards from you and then you draw from me."

She was insistent. "No, you pulls from me."

Annette, who seemed to me the only child in the group who might really belong in an EMH group, asked, "Do you smoke, teachah?"

"No, I don't smoke," I said as I pulled a card.

She said, "I bet you don't even know how to smoke a reefer, do you?"

One of the quietest and shabbiest of the boys, Tyrone, said, "You gotta fix your tongue different to smoke a reefer. Den yo eyes git red and yuh gits drunk. I knows how to smoke reefers 'cause my uncle gots a whole drawer full o' pot." To me, he said, "Want me to bring you some?"

"No, thank you, Tyrone."

Cynthia, who had the long hair that the kids called 'good hair,' and bangs that curled under in a roll, ran her hand through my hair. "Miss Dee, how come colored folks can't have hair like yourn?"

I said, "People are different. I inherited this kind of hair from my parents, just like you inherited your hair from your parents."

Chapter Nine

"Oh, Miss Dee, if I had a comb, I bet I could make yo hair sho look pretty. You got a comb?"

I got my comb, took the band from my hair, and Cynthia started combing. "I bet I could make yo hair have a natural, just like colored folks." She started backcombing my long, straight, gray hair.

One of the girls said, "Let me see teachah's rubber band."

Annette frowned and said, "Teachahs don't weah rubbah bands, dey weah pony-tail holders."

Cynthia spoke wistfully and dreamily as she combed. "My hair on my pussy is just like dis."

Eric said, "Ain't so neither."

Cynthia said softly, "It hang out from under my clothes, it so long."

Annette said, "Colored folks is lucky, dey got two ways to press dey hair. White folks ain't got but one way to press dey hair. Dey jist lay dey head on de ironing board, and dey gits somebody else to iron it for 'em."

"How you know dat?" Cynthia asked.

"'Cause I seen 'em do it lots of times."

Cynthia walked around in front of me and looked at her work. "Let me take yo glasses off." As I handed them to her, she said, "Ya'll look! Don't teachah look pretty! Oh, Miss Dee, you oughta wear yo hair home like dis. If yo husband could see you look like dis, he'd say, 'Oh, baby, yo sho looks fine!'"

I was almost afraid to look in a mirror. Two braids stuck up on top front, and my long straight hair ratted and sticking out all over. Yes, she had given me a natural.

87

Teachah Don't Know Nothin'

She asked, "Do you let yo hair go long when you go to bed at night?"

"Sometimes," I said.

She ran her hand over my hair and said, "Oh, I bet yo husband like dat. Do yo husband evah kiss you?'

"Yes."

"And do you kiss him back?"

"Yes."

Ruby said, "Miss Dee, do you and yo husban' evah have sex?" I didn't know what to say so I pretended not to hear. Foolish me! She yelled, "Miss Dee! Didn't ya hear me? I said do you evah have sex with yo husban'? Do it hurt when he put it in?"

I tried to get busy with other work. "Miss Dee, when yo husband on top o' you, and he stick it in, do you say 'Oh, dat hurt?' Is dat what you say?" She was getting angry.

I was embarrassed and had no idea what to say. My reply was, "Ruby, some things are personal and I don't talk about them. I'm from the South and we don't talk about sex."

Cynthia got me off the hook. She said, "Stop talking like dat, Ruby. Don't you know white folks don't talk about things like dat?"

How right Cynthia was. I didn't talk about things like that. Sex had been a taboo subject as I was growing up, and I still couldn't talk about it.

Cynthia handed my glasses back and said, "Miss Dee, what you do when yo husband hits you?"

"He doesn't hit me, Cynthia."

"But what would you do if he did? Would you hit him back?"

Chapter Nine

"No, I'd probably just walk out and leave him."

Very quietly, and with a mature, knowing sound to her voice, she said, "Well, dat's stupid!"

Tiny little Ruby asked, "Who do yo kids help when yo has a fight with yo husband?"

I replied, "We don't fight, but if we did, how could the kids help?"

"When my mothah and my fathah has a fight, I kicks my fathah on the legs and hits him on the head with a Coke bottle. If yo husband did hit you, what would you do? Is you afraid of him?"

"Sure, I'd be afraid of him. He's bigger than I am."

Ruby laughed, "Oh, Miss Dee! Don't you know biggah don't count in fights?"

Willie asked, "In yo neighborhood, do you have ganes?"

I didn't understand the word. "Ganes? What's that?"

Willie said in an irritated voice, "Gangs, like de Stones, and de D's. At night-time dey have bang-out, shoot-out, and de police come. Last time de police kilt a man. Ever'body gots to belong to a gang. 1900 building, dats de Stones. 1800 building, dats de D's."

I knew nothing about gangs and thought "D's" was spelled 'Dees.' Years later I learned that Stones were the Black P-Stones, and the D's were Disciples.

One day Willie and Tyrone came in from recess and began name-calling. Tyrone said, " You sucks yo daddy's cock!"

Willie answered, "Yes, and I sucks my mothah's pussy. Now I got you one, and I got you two, and I's gonna git you three. Watch dis." He unzipped the fly on his pants. "Look

Teachah Don't Know Nothin'

dare! It's all clean in dare. Evahthing you see in dare is all clean. Now, I's got you number three. What you gonna say?"

He turned around, walked away, and the episode was finished. Willie had won at the game of "Playing the Dozens," and he probably didn't know it was a game. The strategy in the game is to outdo your opponent by saying the worst thing you can think of. As in this case, the winner ends the game and everyone is satisfied, or, the loser gets angry and a fight breaks out. Years later I learned about this competitive game called "Playing the Dozens."

Willie had bragged about his clean body because he was clean that day. He and the others in the class had full baths so seldom that they were conscious of their cleanliness when they were clean. They were the most impoverished and least cared-for of all the children I'd seen.

Besides their unclean bodies, they had with them always the anger they carried inside. Most of the children at Suder, including these, were emotionally needy and handicapped in their social skills. The ones in this EMH room were not well enough adjusted socially to fit into regular classes.

Once, when Eric was running around the room, throwing his book and papers on the floor, and I insisted he sit down and get to work, he said, "I swear, somebody gonna git you when you walk out de doh!" Then he said, "Now, gimme some paper. I'm gonna work." Whenever the kids got angry with me, they remarked about what somebody was going to do to me. One time the tires on my car were flattened, and another time, someone poured sugar in the gas tank. My leather jacket was stolen when I left it in the office, along

Chapter Nine

with my car keys. I took the train to Lake Forest, where my husband worked, and he was afraid of coming in that neighborhood after dark to get the car.

Taking things that belonged to someone else seemed to be the norm, and the kids didn't usually get upset about losing something. In fact, they respected the one who was smart enough to steal from them.

But that wasn't always the case. One day Willie brought a $5 food stamp to school and laid it on his desk and it disappeared. Nobody took things from Willie. After we'd searched the room and still couldn't find it, he looked at me with tears streaming down his face, his fists tight, and screamed, "It's all yo fault! If you'd a put it in yo titties like you's 'sposed to, dey couldn't a got it!"

There was no way I could let Willie see my laughter. I couldn't keep my face straight, so I turned to the board and began writing.

"Yo mama!" he yelled at me.

I continued writing, ignoring him.

"Yo sistah!" I still ignored him and he continued. "Yo aunty!" He waited a few seconds and yelled, "Yo grandmama!"

Still getting no response, he said, "Yo's a hoe!" I knew hoe meant whore.

He was getting desperate. "Don't you know what I's a'callin' you? Yo's a prostitute!"

Finally I knew the meaning of 'Yo mama'! It meant your mother was a prostitute! I'd waited years to learn that. I put my arms around Willie and hugged him. "Thank you, Willie," I said. Since I didn't respond to Willie's 'Yo mama,'

Teachah Don't Know Nothin'

he called me a prostitute. Evidently, even though many of the girls and women were prostitutes, it was not a respectable vocation.

I wondered how the adults in the lives of these children treated them, and what their apartments were like. They kept telling me, "You ain't nevah been in no project." My ignorance was apparent to the children in every school. Often when I made a comment or asked a question, the kids would say, "You ain't never been in no projects." I was putting my purse in the locker when one of the children said, "Can't take no purse like dat in da projects." In a previous school the kids had told me I shouldn't get on the El going south with a purse like mine, somebody would take it. I ask if she would take it from me. "Well," she said thoughtfully, "somebody gonna take it. Wouldn't you want somebody you know to have it?"

Five buildings made up their project. They lived in the last building to the west. I came to hate projects while I was there, for I had never seen children so disturbed emotionally. They acted angry, tough, mean, and scared. Every morning was the same: I faced the task of trying to calm and relax angry kids so they might, maybe, learn a little.

When I mentioned Suder School to a teacher from another school in the Horner projects, she said the project buildings were rated by the type of people living in them, and that the one where Suder kids lived ranked five, the worst of all. "You know," she said, " people sort of draw others like themselves, and that building's got the worst."

Chapter Nine

Usually the kids calmed down and listened when I read them a story. And they liked for us to have talk sessions when they could ask me questions. Maybe in the short time I was there, a few of them learned a little. I felt sure, no matter how much effort I put into academics, the amount learned was minimal, if any. The Suder kids seemed to be doing well if all they did was make it from day to day without getting hurt or killed.

Chapter Ten

One afternoon at Suder when it was time to leave for the day, one of the boys pulled my hair. As I turned toward him, the ruler in my hand hit his hand, making a cut that began to bleed.

What had I done?

He began threatening to sue.

I had hurt a child. I had never hurt a child before. What kind of a teacher was I? I had swung around with a reflexive action, but no matter how the injury had happened I went home upset and feeling guilty.

My husband had never wanted me to teach in the inner city schools. He took this opportunity to insist, "You're not going back. It's not safe there, and you know it. Now maybe you'll understand what I've been telling you all along. This is enough!"

I didn't go back.

Teachah Don't Know Nothin'

The principal said if I didn't want to come back to Suder he'd get me a job in another school. But the pain inside was too big. I figured I didn't belong in teaching. As much as I enjoyed children, I didn't belong in teaching if I could hurt a child.

I couldn't stay at home, though. I got a real estate license and sold one lot. I got licensed in insurance and sold two policies. I worked with a company that helped people invest their money, but I wasn't good at it. I worked as cashier at an upscale restaurant for three months and think I might have balanced the cash register with the receipts two or three times. It seemed there was nothing I could do well.

The only thing I liked to do was teach. When I considered teaching again, a voice in my head would say what I'd often heard: Those who can't do anything else, teach.

I seemed to be one of those who couldn't do anything else. Within a few years I began substituting again.

The boy whose hand I cut did sue, and was awarded $2,000.

Shortly after returning to Chicago schools as a substitute, I was sent to Simpson School for Pregnant Girls, in the elementary section, grades seven and eight, girls 11 to 15 years of age. It was hard for me to believe that all these little girls were pregnant or had just had a baby. They came to Simpson when they discovered they were pregnant and came back for a few months after the baby was born.

Chapter Ten

The first day the social worker, principal, and assistant principal kept coming by the door and peering into the room. I was unaware that they were searching for a full-time teacher for the other class of the same age girls. Cloyanne, the social worker, told me a number of times that she was the one responsible for my being asked to take the job. She said she walked by the classroom a few times, then went to the principal and said, "She belongs here. Keep her."

That's how I began my years at Simpson, where I discovered how much I enjoyed working with older children. My training as a reading consultant allowed me to teach all grades, so I applied and got a high school teaching certificate, and quickly began taking classes to qualify for a BD (Behavior Disordered) certificate. Simpson was a special education school for BD girls.

In most schools, grades seven and eight were called junior high school, but at Simpson these grades were referred to as the elementary section. One of the girls said to me early on, "Miss Dee, we don't like to be called 'elementary.'"

I asked, "Is there a reason you don't like the word elementary?" I thought she would say because it sounded like they were young children.

She said, "Sho is. You know, 'Elementary, my dear Watson, elementary.'"

I laughed and said they were junior high students and should be called that. I didn't tell her I was also thinking that these girls were no more 'behavior disordered' than other kids in inner city schools. They were pregnant, most

Teachah Don't Know Nothin'

of them from black inner city areas, and most of them scored below grade level on achievement tests.

Of course, these younger girls were apt to be lower achieving and troubled, or they wouldn't have gotten themselves pregnant at such an early age. Girls in the high school section, where I would later work, were often good students.

The school was housed in a rambling, old, former Catholic school building that was not air-conditioned, and we had school during the summer. One afternoon Loretta pulled her red bandanna headband off, pushed her hair back with her hands, and said, "It's hot in here, Miss Dee. But I don't be sweatin'. It can be in the hundreds and I don't sweat. You can ask my mama. I don't never sweat. The only time was that day when I had that baby. My clothes and my head was soakin' wet. My hair was nappy. My back was wet wid all that sweat."

Little air came through the open windows, and although I brought in a few fans, they helped little when the temperature was high. During our eight-week summer school, Chicago's temperatures often topped the 100-degree mark.

Because my name had been difficult for children to pronounce, I suggested they call me "Miss Dee." After a few months the principal called me into her office and told me this was not appropriate - said it reminded her of slave days. She was an older black woman whose grandparents had been slaves.

Chapter Ten

I told the children they were to call me Mrs. Oglesby, wrote Mrs. Oglesby on the board, and reminded them often, but they still called me Miss Dee.

The principal also said the personal lives of the girls had no place in school, so I made an effort to keep things in my classroom totally academic, but it was impossible. I often wasn't aware of a difference between personal and academic. To me, any reading and writing the students did was academic, and I thought they learned more from subjects related to their lives than they did from material that had no meaning for them.

Claudette was the youngest student I taught at Simpson. She had "just made" her eleventh birthday and ran around like a five- or six-year-old. There she was, pregnant, and in a classroom with seventh- and eighth-graders, with no idea about what it meant to be pregnant. A few ten-year olds had attended Simpson School over the years, but the youngest in my class was eleven.

I overheard one of the girls say she had known she wouldn't get pregnant when she first had sex, because she hadn't started menstruating yet. The teachers often remarked, "Babies having babies," and the girls often said to each other, "You just a baby havin' a baby."

The phrasing Claudette used about her birthday was common: "I just made eleven." Other examples were, "I want to make a boy." "I want to make a girl." "She has made three months."

It wasn't unusual for the girls to talk about being hit by their boyfriends. Judging by their remarks, I'd say they were proud of their bruises, that they thought the bruises

Teachah Don't Know Nothin'

showed that the boys loved them. One day Betty showed the bruise on her arm to Loretta and said, "Look what my man did to me last night."

Loretta said, "I let my man hit me a little, but not hard."

Hazel asked Lashon, "What do you do when your boyfriend hits you?"

Lashon looked up from her work and said, "Well, I just sit there and hang my head down and cry. One time I forgot and hit him back and he said, 'What the hell!'"

In the lunchroom one day, a tall, light-skinned fifteen-year-old named Theresa said, "A baby sho look good when they smiles. I look at my baby all the time. Now, Miss Dee, don't a baby look good when she smile, with no teeth? Did you ever see a old man with no teeth and smilin'?"

I agreed with Theresa, and then my attention was diverted to a new girl coming through the door, a high school girl. On both sides of her head was a streak of red hair. She must have felt us watching her, for she put her hands to the sides of her head, as if to hide the red. The principal was walking past my chair. She noticed the new girl too, and said to me in a low voice, "I haven't seen that here in a long time. That's gang, you know." I didn't know.

The girls at my table kept talking. Annette, who wore round-shaped glasses and had round cheeks and a pretty grin said, "My boyfriend went to the police station and they said, 'What's yo name?' He said, 'My name is Joe, I fucked a hoe, that's how I make all my mothahfuckin' doh.'"

Cheryl finished drinking her milk, wiped her mouth on her sleeve, and said with a twinkle in her eye, "How about this one? One day Mr. Goodbar wanted a Bitta Honey, and

Chapter Ten

he took her behind a car on Fifth Avenue. He stuck his Butter Finger in her Kit Kat. She kicked him in his Butter Nuts, and that was all till his Pay Day."

Annette pushed her tray aside and grinned her big round smile. She said, "Where'd you get that? Did you make it up?"

"Uh-huh," Cheryl said. She was the agitator in the group, with big eyes and a big mouth - solid, husky, nothing dainty about her.

Ann propped her elbows on the table, with hands holding her chin as she said, "When my baby grow up, if he be a boy, he gonna be a pimp."

Ethel lifted her long-lashed eyes and said, " I want my baby to be a pimp, too."

Lashon said, "My baby gonna be a football player."

The girls never mentioned any other futures for their sons than those two. If a son was to be successful, the girls assumed, he had to become either a pimp or successful in sports.

I asked, "Why would girls do what a pimp asked them to do?"

Lashon said. "'Cause dey scared o' men, dat's why. An' da men don't ask nothin'. Dey tells!"

Ethel said, "My pimp scared o' me."

I was curious. "I thought the pimp asked a girl if he could be her pimp," I said.

Little Loretta said, "Ain't nobody gonna put me out there. My mama gonna kill dat man."

Cheryl shot back, "Yo mama gonna fool you one day."

101

Teachah Don't Know Nothin'

Loretta jerked her head around. "My mama ain't gonna do shit."

Cheryl kept feeding the fire. "She gonna say if you old enough to go out there and git fucked, you old enough to fuck, or sump'n like dat."

"My mama done put her words down. She say if evah a nigger try to put me out there, and if I get out there, she gonna come out there and kick my ass and break my arm and break my leg, and she gonna kill dat motahfucker."

Cheryl said, "She might kill you too if she doin' all dat."

"What you sayin'? Like you sayin' my mama don't care nothin' 'bout me?"

Cheryl turned and said something to Cynthia.

Loretta asked Cynthia, "What she say? She say somethin' about my mama?"

Cynthia grinned. "Why, she say you been fuckin' ever since you was seven."

"Ever since I was seven? Girl, don't you know I didn't know nothin' 'bout no nigger when I was seven years old? If you believe that, Cheryl, I ain't gonna talk to you no mo'."

Cheryl wasn't ready to quit. "It could be true and you just denying it."

Loretta said, "You so damn stupid!" She gave me a quick glance and said, " I'm sorry I said dat, Miss Dee." Turning back to Cheryl, she said, "Anyway, if I did start fuckin' when I was seven, it's my business, and I wouldn't be ashamed to tell it. One time when I was little I ask my mama, 'Mama, what is a dick?' She say, 'Girl, get yo fancy ass out o' here.'"

102

Chapter Ten

Cheryl looked at me. "They growin' up too fast, Miss Dee."

Ethel was mad. "I bet if you said I fucked my daddy you'd believe that shit. My mama'd kick my ass, hersef."

Cheryl kept on. "She'd say, den and again, I'd just let him fuck her. And she'd say you was hoe'n on Madison."

"You just a bitch. I wouldn't never get out there and sell my ass for no mothahfucker. But that's my business."

They kept on Playing the Dozens for awhile, just like the boys had. Making up and saying the worst things they could think of to say, and nobody paying any real attention to most of it.

Ethel was popping her gum so loud it seemed to echo in the room. I said, "Ethel, either take that gum out or chew with your mouth shut."

She replied, "Last time my math teacher told me to take out my gum, you know where I put it? I put it in her hair."

Cheryl said, "You bettah not do nothin' to Miss Dee. We take care of her here. You'll have to fight us all if you do something to Miss Dee."

On Valentine's Day we gave a program for the rest of the school. The girls wrote love poems, then found a record of soft organ music to use in the background. They dressed in their best shoes and hose and dresses, most of them red, and spoke as though they were professionals. I was so proud of them my eyes were full of tears. Here are three of the poems they wrote.

Teachah Don't Know Nothin'

LOVE IS
Sometimes you can't really explain or show people
How much you love them.
A lot of people say they love you,
But you really don't know how much they love you
Until you are down and really need that person,
So you see how much they love you.
Love speaks for itself.
Sometimes you can't really believe when a person tells you that.
You just have to wait until you really need them
And then you see how much that person really loves you.
        By Loretta

LOVE FOR YOUR CHILD
Love for your baby is not letting anything
Get in the way of the feeling you have for your child,
And not letting it go around being hungry all the time.
Love for your child is something no one can take away from you.
It's something that will stay forever.
It's taking care of a sore knee when he falls to the ground,
Giving a birthday party and watching
While he blows out the candles on his cake.
It's looking back a year ago
And looking at the first fall and the first step,

Chapter Ten

And helping him write his own name,
And buying clothes for a holiday,
And watching on Christmas
While he plays with all the toys.
That's what love for your child means.
    By Cheryl

LOVE IS A FEELING
Love is a feeling deep within your heart and soul
in which you devote yourself to the people
that are special to you.
Love is so many different things that you don't really
Know when it's there or gone.
Love seems to be an indefinable word.
Love will make you do things that you'd never think
of doing.
Although you know it might be wrong, you do it,
Just for the person who you love.
Love is a nice feeling, and if everyone
Had real true love in their hearts today,
This would be a beautiful, wonderful place.
    By Lashon

Naming babies was a big deal for the girls. Usually they tried to make up a name, so it would be unusual. One of them named her baby Tanqueray like Tanqueray Gin.

When Ethel was about to have her second baby, Cheryl said, "Gloria and Ethel have the same baby daddy."

Teachah Don't Know Nothin'

Loretta said, " No, Ethel's first baby by Bebe. Then Gloria snatched Bebe from Ethel. Ethel not pregnant by Bebe this time. I'm gonna name my baby She-li-ta-ki La-cole for a girl, how you like that?"

"How you gonna spell it?"

"Just like this." She spelled it, and said, "And Lavell for a boy."

Althea said, "If you hangin' high, it's a boy. If you hangin' low, it's a girl."

Lashon said, "Hazel, you'se a hoe. I didn't know you was a hoe." She used the same tone of voice as if she were saying, Hazel, John is your brother. I didn't know John was your brother.

Cheryl reached for her workbook and flashed her big grin at me. She said, "It's dem hot-tailed girls that end up having the second baby."

After Hazel's second baby was born, and before she went back to her regular school, she was afraid to leave school to get on the bus because her pimp waited outside for her. Her mother or sister came to school to meet her each day to protect her from him. She wrote the following:

WHAT I THINK ABOUT PROSTITUTION.

I think prostitution is very stupid. For a woman to work the street she must have a body on her. But I think a woman is crazy. She don't got no sense. She got no way to get away from this pimp. Everywhere she go that pimp is going to follow her for her money. She going to be afraid so she going to give it to him. The pimp beat the women if they don't have all their money. They get call out of their name (called bad

Chapter Ten

names) and everything. Some even get killed because they don't have all the pimp money.

Prostitutes need all the help they can get to get off the street to get away from the pimp and to get away from the dope. It will be nice to clean up the street, get the prostitute off the street, to stop the dope dealers and we all need to do something about the pimp. They should not be able to get gas in their car because if they get the gas to put in their car they get where they are going with the girl. Pimps don't need no gas or money. They all need to be locked up for life for what they do to the women. Black women, we need to fight for women wright. We have our wright. We must stand up for todays world and tomorrow's world. Hazel, 13.

Once, when the girls were dancing to music on the radio, I watched Hazel dance. She danced as if she were in a different world. Every cell in her body danced. That day I decided for my next life I'd come back as Hazel Hightower and do nothing but dance a whole lifetime.

I often wondered what my life would have been like if I'd been born with black skin. Many times I looked in the mirror and imagined seeing a black face. Sometimes I thought I'd have been able to work better with the children if my skin had been black. I didn't ever wish for a black face, but I'd have been happy to have bigger lips.

Chapter Eleven

One day we were working on making a bulletin board with the names of the girls' babies. They were drawing and designing name cards and Cheryl noticed the design I was helping Ethel make and said, "Look, yawl, they be doing somethin' real freakish. Miss Dee, why you writin' her baby name so te-ren-dish? You know what I mean, so terrific."

Ethel said, "Cheryl, how come you so jealous?"

"I'm not jealous."

"You act like it."

Cheryl said in a jeering tone, "Ours is on a lil' blue card like dis, and she puttin' yours on a big card with designs all ovah it."

Laticia said, "'Cause she got a big name. She gonna give her baby eight names."

Cheryl said, "My baby got mo' names than dat. She got Cheryl, Black, Brown, Williams, Glass, Angela, Faulkner,

Teachah Don't Know Nothin'

and Jada Brown. Ever' time I take her to the doctor, he say, 'Jada Brown. Someday I'm gonna see Jada Brown up in lights.' He a black doctor. He so fine."

Ethel said, "Jada Brown is a phoney-ass name."

Gloria, who was usually quiet, said, "I ain't gonna put my baby name up there. Anybody can take my baby name. I don't got to put it up there."

I said, "Gloria, you don't have to put your baby's name up there, but I think nobody here would take the name you have for your baby. Maybe you could make a book about your baby and put the name in there."

Cheryl rolled her big eyes and said, "Oh, Miss Dee, you always thinkin' up somethin'."

Cheryl said, "Yawl shouldn't put your hopes up too high. I didn't know what I was gonna name my baby till after she was born, 'cause I wanted to make sure my baby was gonna be there, and be alive when I name her. I was worried about if my baby was gonna live. I wanted to know if she was okay. She was a little red baby girl. And she could see. I like hot sauce, and you know hot sauce can blind your baby. I looked at her and I said, Jada Brown, that's your name. She went home in all pink. She was cleaner than the Board of Health."

Laticia changed the subject. "My mama took me to the hospital yesterday when I fell. She say, 'Girl, you ain't got nothin' bettah to do? Now I have to take you to the hospital.' She took me to the emergency ward, but we had to hunt for our green card befo' we went."

I asked, "What's a green card?"

"We got a green card fo' the doctor, so we can see him."

Chapter Eleven

"But not for the hospital?"

"Yeah, that's the hospital, too. I went to the emergency ward, and they wrote my name down and took me in a room and the doctor look at my hand, and clean it in a hurry, den de nurse give me a tetanus shot for lock jaw, dat's the reason my teeth hurt. Den the doctor shot me again. He was deadening it. Den he put the stitches in it. That doctor made me so mad. He said, 'You didn't have nothin' else bettah to do?'"

I was curious about how welfare worked. "You didn't have to pay for anything?"

"No, the Board of Health paid for it."

"What about your glasses?"

"The kind of glasses you got, I have to pay for them. But just regular glasses, I don't have to pay - "

Cheryl interrupted. "ADC is what it's called - means, 'After Daddy cut out.'"

Laticia kept going with her explanation. "See, you can get on Aid, it's ADC rather, when you tired o' workin' and you don't want to work no mo'. If you get on Aid, you can't work, 'cause they be takin' care of you. You can work for cash and they don't know it. Yo baby can git on it now, though. Even if yo mothah workin' you can still git on Aid."

"And your mother's working?" I asked.

"She was a bus driver, before I got pregnant."

Lashon interjected, "My boyfriend works, his mother works, her boyfriend and her husband work."

Teachah Don't Know Nothin'

I continued the conversation with Laticia. "You mean your mother quit work and went on Aid to take care of your baby?"

"She been on Aid. They just didn't know she was workin', cause if they found out she was workin' they'd a took her off Aid. Understand?"

"Yes," I said, "she just didn't let them know she was working."

"Yeah. You see, she had to git enough money to support all three o' us, and pay the rent. But, see, we movin' on 89th with this old lady - she can't walk. Both her legs got cut off. So we movin' over there and all we gotta pay is $140 for the rent and the lights and stuff like that. My mama gonna stay with her and take care of her and take care of my baby. And then we gonna be closer to the bus line. But I don't want to go over there. My baby father live close there and he'll be wantin' to come over there every day, or want me to come to his house every day."

"You don't want to?" I asked.

"I don't go over there every day now. I'm gonna have to make up some excuse, and he always catch me when I'm lying."

I said, "I thought you were in love with Melvin."

"I am, but not to jump in his box. I love him, but I don't jump in his box. If you let a niggah know that you easy goin', I mean easy to go places with him and stuff, then he say, 'Oh, baby, come on.'" She shrugged her shoulders and said, "And like a fool, I go."

"Won't he get somebody else to go with him?"

Chapter Eleven

"Hunh-uh. Well, I don't know, he could. But I'll put my trust in him. He got my trust. If he mess it up, it's ovah. I told him, I said, 'Melvin, if you don't want me, I can get off now.' And he say, 'Baby, if I don't see you Saturday, I have to pick.' And what he mean by dat, I don't know."

"He's still got your picture?" I asked.

"Yeah, a picture of me and my baby."

"Does Melvin help support your baby?"

"Dat nigger? You think I'm gonna ask him for money? Dat's charity. I'm gonna take care of my baby with Aid."

"Do you think it fair that I'm paying taxes to help pay for your baby?"

"If you don't want us to have it, what you got it for?"

Good question, I thought.

Ethel said she had to come to school late in the mornings during the summer, because on her way to school she had to go by her church and sign up for the CETA program.

I said, "I thought the CETA program was to pay for summer work. When do you work?"

"I don't work. I just sign in befo' I come to school, and go by and sign again when I get out of school. Dat way I get paid to come to school."

Many times the students talked about schemes for getting money from assistance programs.

The girls decided to write a play for the Christmas program and call it "The Christmas Baby." They worked on the play for weeks, getting everything just right. Although my typing was terrible, I typed it at home on ditto carbons and ran it off at school. I hated those dittos. Correcting mistakes was almost impossible, I never knew how many good copies I'd get from a carbon, and the purple print was usually difficult to read. I'd have purple all over myself while I was trying to get the ditto on the drum just right. I did manage to get the pages typed and run off well enough for them to read.

THE CHRISTMAS BABY

ACT 1. The scene is located in Ann Galloway's home in the kitchen. Ann is a girl 13 years old who has two older sisters. They live with their mother. Ann is sitting at the kitchen table when her sisters come in the room.

Ann: Can I talk to you for a minute?

Gloria: Hold on, Betty. OK, Ann, what do you want to talk to us about?

Ann: Well, I think I'm pregnant.

Betty: Pregnant!!! Why do you think you is pregnant?

Ann: Because I skipped my menstruation period last month.

Gloria: Who is you pregnant by?

Ann: Sylvester.

Gloria: Sylvester? Who's that?

Ann: He's that dude that plays football, got light skin.

Betty: How old is he?

Ann: 21.

Betty: How old did you tell him you was?

Ann: 16.

Gloria: What's Mama gonna say about this?

Ann: She's probably gonna be upset, just like you are. I don't care what Mama say, this is my baby.

Chapter Eleven

Gloria: I'm not upset. I'm just telling you, 'cause she gonna be upset.

Ann: I know, but what am I gonna do?

Betty: Let's go to the hospital.

Ann: I don't want to go to the hospital, 'cause it's embarrassing to go to the hospital with all them people staring.

Betty: You gonna have to go anyway, 'cause Mama gonna find out sooner or later.

Ann: All right then.

ACT 2:

Announcer: Then next day at the hospital, Ann and her sisters appear at the reception desk in the clinic of the hospital.

Ann: Hello. May I see the doctor, please?

Nurse: What do you want to see the doctor about?

Ann: I want to take a rabbit test because I think I'm pregnant.

Nurse: What is your name?

Ann: Ann Galloway.

Nurse: Just have a seat over there. The doctor will be with you in a minute.

Ann: Thank you.

Ann: (to her sisters) What am I gonna tell Mama?

Betty: Just sit down and tell her you're pregnant.

Ann: You know how upset Mama gets. I don't want to hurt Mama.

Betty: You are not going to hurt her, 'cause she may hurt you first.

Ann: Well, I think you know better than me.

Teachah Don't Know Nothin'

Nurse: Ann Galloway, step in this room please. The doctor will be with you in a minute.

Announcer: Ann walks into the next room and sits down. The nurse enters shortly.

Nurse: Hello, I'm the nurse, Mrs. Foster. Now, Ann, tell me, when was your last menstrual period?

Ann: March the 20th.

Nurse: I am going to give you a physical examination. First I am going to weigh you, then take your blood pressure, blood tests and urine test. Then I want you to take off all your clothes and put on this gown and get on the table so we can give you a pelvic examination.

Announcer: After her examination, Ann was told that her due date is on Christmas day. The nurse gave Ann another appointment date. After Ann leaves, the nurse calls Ann's mother to give her the bad news.

ACT 3.

Announcer: This act takes place in the Galloway home, again in the kitchen.

Gloria: When that boy comes to this house this evening, I'm going to tell him you ain't nothing but 13 years old.

Ann: I don't care what you tell him. He'll still love me.

Gloria: That's what you think.

Betty: What's your friends going to say about this?

Ann: Well. . .

Gloria: What's MY friends gonna say about this? That's what I want to know.

Mrs. Galloway: And what's MY friends gonna say about this? A thirteen year old girl going out letting everybody get under her dress.

Chapter Eleven

Betty: I don't see how anybody would want you, as ugly as you are.

Mrs. Galloway: Hush, now, that's enough.

Betty: We didn't tell her to get caught in the hallway. . .

Ann: It wasn't in the hallway. It was in bed.

Mrs. Galloway: Is Sylvester working?

Ann: No, he's not out of high school yet.

Mrs. Galloway: Then how do you think you're going to make a life for this baby?

Ann: I don't know. I was thinking about getting an abortion.

Announcer: Mrs. Galloway is angry.

Mrs. Galloway: I don't believe in abortions, and you know that.

Ann: Well, then, Mama, what am I going to do?

Mrs. Galloway: Well, we'll see as time goes by.

Announcer: Ann leaves the room and goes upstairs.

Mrs. Galloway: Gloria, why didn't you girls tell me that Ann was pregnant?

Gloria: Well, Mama, Ann says I got a big mouth and always talk too much, and she said, This time, please don't tell Mama. I don't want to hurt her. So I didn't tell you.

Mrs. Galloway: This is very serious, Gloria. You girls should have told me about it.

Announcer: Gloria and Betty leave the kitchen and go upstairs. Mrs. Galloway puts her head down on the table. As time goes by there is a knock on the door.

(Knock, knock, knock)

Mrs. Galloway: Come in.

Sylvester: I'm Sylvester, Ann's boyfriend.

Teachah Don't Know Nothin'

Mrs. Galloway: The father of Ann's baby, you mean. Come in and sit down. You're just the guy I want to talk to.

Sylvester: Ann's going to have a baby! I didn't know Ann was going to have a baby.

Mrs. Galloway: Well, now you do. I want to know how could you do this to my baby? She's just a baby. How could you do this to her?

Sylvester: But I didn't do it to her, she told me to.

Mrs. Galloway: She told you to! (Yelling) Ann Galloway, come down here!

Announcer: Ann didn't come right away. She was afraid to face her mother and Sylvester together. Then Mrs. Galloway yelled louder.

Mrs. Galloway: Ann Galloway, bring your butt down here this minute, girl!

Ann: (shyly) Hello, Sylvester.

Sylvester: Ann, are you pregnant?

Ann: Yes.

Sylvester: Oh, Ann! And you ain't nothing but 16, and I ain't nothing but 21. We ain't even finished school yet.

Mrs. Galloway: Hush, boy! Where did you get that lie from? Ann ain't nothing but 13 years old!

Sylvester: She's 13?

Mrs. Galloway: Ann is 13 years old. She was born in 1964.

Sylvester: Ann, why didn't you tell me you wasn't nothing but 13 and had me breaking you in? And, Ann, why didn't you tell me you were pregnant?

Ann: I was goin' to. . .

Chapter Eleven

Mrs. Galloway: You were going to tell HIM? But you weren't going to tell me? And why not?

Ann: Well, I didn't think it would hurt him as much as it would you.

Sylvester: Ann, why didn't you go and get some birth control pills?

Ann: I didn't know. I didn't know I would get pregnant.

Sylvester: You didn't?

Ann: No, I didn't. Besides that, it's all your fault.

Sylvester: How is it my fault? I didn't make you lay down there.

Ann: Yes, you did.

Mrs. Galloway: He can't make you do nothing.

Ann: OK, Mama, then, just say I was willing to.

Mrs.: Galloway: Ann, why didn't you tell me ahead of time?

Ann: I didn't know, Mama.

Act 4.

Announcer: As time goes by, Ann is in the labor room of Cook County Hospital. It is Christmas Day. Her mother enters.

Mrs. Galloway: My baby! Look at her! Can you bear with it, Ann?

Ann: Oh, no, Mama, it hurts too much!

Mrs. Galloway: (Praying) Please, Lord, don't let my baby suffer so long.

Ann: Oh, Mama, it hurts.

Mrs. Galloway: Now, Baby, just know this won't last long. Then you'll have your little baby.

Teachah Don't Know Nothin'

Ann: Oh, Mama, I don't want a baby! I don't want a baby!

Mrs. Galloway: I know, Ann. But you can't do nothing about that now. Most everybody don't want the baby when they're in labor. Only way you can get out of this is to have this baby just as easy as you can. Now, the next time you feel a contraction coming on, you just let go of your body, and let that baby push, and you hold tight to my hand.

Ann: Now, Mama, now.

Mrs. Galloway: Now, take a deep breath and relax and just let that little baby push himself right out of there.

Ann: That didn't hurt so much.

Mrs. Galloway: When you just let your body go with it, that little baby wants to get out of there and he'll push himself out. Just don't you tighten up and fight it, cause if you do, that tries to hold on to him. Don't fight it, just let him go.

Ann: Hold on again, Mama.

Mrs. Galloway: Now you are helping to push that little baby out, a little Christmas baby.

Ann: I'm so glad he's coming on Christmas Day.

Announcer: As time goes by the nurse enters and puts her hand on Ann's stomach and turns to Mrs. Galloway.

Nurse: Mrs. Galloway, I must ask you to leave the room for a few minutes.

Announcer: As time goes by the nurse examines Ann and then tells Mrs. Galloway she may come back into the room.

Nurse: She's about ready to deliver, so now we'll have to take her to the delivery room.

Chapter Eleven

Mrs. Galloway: You must be going to have a big baby, Ann. Big babies are easier to push out than little babies.

Ann: I'll see you later, Mama.

Announcer: Mrs. Galloway kisses Ann and goes home. As time goes by Ann is in the delivery room.

Doctor Linda: Now, Ann, the baby is ready to be delivered. When the nurse puts her hands on your stomach and says push, you push down and help the baby get out.

Ann: OK.

Nurse: Push, now.

Dr. Linda: That's great, Ann. You're doing just perfect. Now, I'm going to give you a shot so we can cut you just a little so you won't tear. You're having a big baby. There, did you feel that?

Ann: Not much.

Dr. Linda: You're doing fine, Ann. I can see the baby's head now. Now, push again. Here it comes.

Ann: Oh, Oh.

BABY CRIES.

Dr. Linda: Oh, Ann, you have a beautiful, perfect baby boy. I didn't even have to spank him to get him to cry. Here, Nurse, wipe him off a little and give Ann her baby.

Nurse: Here, Ann, now you can hold your baby.

Ann: My little baby boy, little Sylvester.

Announcer: Mrs. Galloway dropped the phone and rushed to Ann's room.

Ann: Mama, it's a boy. Isn't he pretty?

Mrs. Galloway: He's a beautiful baby, Ann. What are you going to name him?

Ann: Sylvester.

Teachah Don't Know Nothin'

Mrs. Galloway: Do you want me to call Sylvester to come over here?

Ann: Yes, Mama, will you call him to come out here?

Announcer: As time goes by Mrs. Galloway calls Sylvester and he comes to the hospital, enters Ann's room and goes to Ann and kisses her.

Sylvester: What's happening? What you been doing? How are you feeling? Fine I hope.

Ann: Yes, Sylvester, I'm doing fine. How do you like our baby boy?

Sylvester: He's a pretty baby. Looks just like his daddy. What did you name him?

Ann: Sylvester, Junior.

Sylvester: That's a good name. He's going to be a mighty fine boy, born on Christmas Day.

Announcer: As time goes by, a bright glow fills the room and when Ann and her mother and Sylvester turn to look toward the window, they are amazed to see there a beautiful woman, dressed in white.

Sylvester: Who are you?

Spirit: I am the Spirit of Christmas of the Future. I have come to tell you that you are very lucky people. Baby Sylvester is going to grow up to be a great man - a leader - and do great things for his people. Your job is to give him lots of love and the best of care. His future is in your hands, so hear me well. Each of you is responsible for helping him grow. Remember: give him lots of love, and special care, for he is a special Christmas present to all of you - everywhere. He is your future Christmases to come!

Chapter Eleven

Announcer: Now, a very special Christmas wish from all of us, including baby Sylvester. Please sing with us . . . "We Wish You A Merry Christmas."

Not only did the girls write the play, they decided everything about it, including who would play the roles. The audience was made up entirely of the staff and students, and audience response was gratifying. There was a lot of laughter, and loud applause. The whole undertaking was a success, from beginning to end.

Abortion was mentioned in the play, but I almost never heard a girl mention that option. The girls seemed thrilled that they were having babies. A baby was something special in a girl's life, something all her own - a real baby doll, a wonderful, wonderful toy.

Shortly before Christmas I found some plants that I thought were poinsettias. They were in the trash at the building where I lived. Their leaves had been stripped, but the plants and roots looked fresh. I planted them in the window planter box and they grew beautifully. During Christmas vacation I saw a picture of that plant in a magazine with the caption, "You could be arrested for growing this plant in your home."

Marijuana!

I got to school early the first day after vacation, pulled all the plants and threw them in the trash, then went to the principal and asked, "Did you know what I was growing in my classroom?"

Teachah Don't Know Nothin'

She grinned and said, "Yes."

I said, "How did you know? I didn't."

"The security guard told me. I was wondering what you were going to do with them."

I felt ignorant and stupid, but mostly thankful that the principal had waited before taking disciplinary action. I did think it strange that the girls hadn't recognized the plants, but drug dealing was not a source of income for most of the kids in the projects at that time. Prostitution and stealing (mostly car theft) were the moneymaking enterprises.

Soon after the holidays were over, the girls were taking off their coats when I heard Cheryl telling about the night before. "Police came in our house and took my brothers - *all* my brothers. Said they stole a car. They didn't do nothin', didn't steal no car. It was their friend who stole it and blamed it on my brothers. They took another boy who was there too - and he just walked in, but they took them all to jail. They still there. Could get my mother thrown out, if CHA (Chicago Housing Authority) finds out about it. They tore up our house. I made them put my clothes back in my drawer. They searched our house without a warrant, trying to find pot or somethin'. I told them, 'You better not hit me.' They can see this big belly. And if I didn't have a big belly, I'd get them for hitting a minor!"

That same morning I admired Annette's bright sweater and was about to compliment her on how pretty she looked. As I got close to her she was saying to one of the girls, "I went with a teacher in my other school, and my girlfriend went with another teacher."

Chapter Eleven

I asked, "Went with him? Where did you go?"
She said, "Oh, Miss Dee, where'd you come from?"

Chapter Twelve

Simpson School was finally torn down to make a parking lot for the Juvenile Detention Center and I was free to choose another school or sign up again for Simpson in the new location. Changing schools was difficult in the Chicago system. If you were a good teacher, your principal didn't want to let you go. If you weren't good, another principal didn't want you. A teacher at Suder told me he became sick to his stomach every morning when he turned the corner onto Washington Boulevard. His name had been on the request-for-transfer list for seven years. But now, because Simpson had been closed, I could choose another school.

While taking classes to become certified to teach Behavior Disordered kids, I heard teachers from Audy, (Juvenile Detention Center) talk about their students. We were sitting in a circular classroom. I sat near the front,

Teachah Don't Know Nothin'

with the Detention Center teachers to my left. The picture of that classroom where I first heard about the school at the Audy Home is deeply etched in my memory, for as I listened, something seemed to click inside me and I thought to myself, I belong there.

From that moment, teaching at the detention center school became an obsessive objective for me. About three years had passed since that moment, but with Simpson's closing, I had at least the option of applying for the Audy School.

Since my first exposure to the "foreign country" of the ghetto culture I had been spellbound by the differences between my own growing-up environment and the world of my students. Since the detention center was one block directly behind Simpson, I had passed it often, and always wondered what the students there were like.

At the time Simpson closed, there were no openings at Audy. I took a position at another school in a special reading program. After one semester that program closed for lack of students, so I checked the Audy listings again. There was one opening, not at Audy itself, but at a branch facility called Bartelme - for high school girls who were wards of the court and lived in group homes, groups of girls lived together in a house with supervision.

Some of the girls had lived most of their lives in foster homes, usually a string of foster homes, but many had been released to the Bartelme group homes from Audy. The students were of three racial groups, about equal in number: black, white and Latino.

Chapter Twelve

One of the group homes housed the most disturbed girls. They were not allowed out without supervision. Girls in the other houses could go home or visit relatives on weekends, and could go out after school. One home housed pregnant girls and girls with babies.

Shortly after I started teaching at Bartelme, some of the girls were talking about why they had been arrested. Ruth, an attractive black girl in a fashionable pantsuit and matching shoes, did not join the conversation. I said, "Ruth, you didn't say why you were in Audy."

She nonchalantly answered, "Assault and battery and murder."

Later I found out she killed her father by hitting him over the head with a chair - because he was abusing her sister.

The girls taught me how to commit crimes - for instance, how to steal cars. Don't even try a Volvo, they said, for you won't be able to "break the steering wheel." Some of the girls told of helping their boyfriends sell drugs. Lachelle said she'd wait on one side of the street while her boyfriend, on the other side, made contact for a sale. He'd signal her, then she'd give the buyer the drug and take the money. She spoke of being in hotel rooms with drug dealers on Saturday nights and counting thousands of dollars, which they packed in brown grocery bags.

In the home for girls with babies, the young mothers were expected to look after their babies, but in some cases they didn't, causing major problems for the social workers. One Monday the talk of the school was about what Janice had done over the weekend. She was a tall, broad-shouldered, overweight white girl who often stirred up

Teachah Don't Know Nothin'

trouble. She had wanted to go out and knew she wouldn't be allowed to take her baby. Somehow she managed to wrap the baby in a plastic bag and sneak it out of the house. The girls expected the baby to suffocate.

A brilliant girl named Penny suffered major emotional problems as well as a drug habit. She was petite, with short curly blond hair, and a radio mouth. I knew that major help had been given to Penny, and still her behavior did not improve. When she came back to school after a three-month stay at a drug rehabilitation center, and still behaved in her usual wild way, I lost my cool and told her when people had done so much to help her, and she didn't appreciate it enough to behave well in school and at her group home, she didn't deserve any help. I told her to leave my classroom and not return until she could at least be courteous.

Penny wasn't the only one who acted ungrateful. The girls often showed almost no appreciation for the help they received. On the contrary, they got angry when they didn't get more, or when they didn't get just what they wanted.

If a girl left her group home without permission, she was "on the run." The social workers might go looking for her, especially if she had been a prostitute, or if they had reason to think a pimp or gang member had taken her. A girl could be on the run a certain number of days and still return to her group home.

Darlene had been on the run for two weeks and needed to make up her work for English. I told her if she could write her life story and make it long enough for two weeks' work, I would take that for her make-up.

Chapter Twelve

Darlene wore thick glasses and always looked clean and neat. She was a light-skinned black girl who wore her hair neatly curled under and snug to her head. She came back in a few days with sixty-eight pages titled "The Lost Love of A Child." Although there was no punctuation, and most words were misspelled or run together, she had obviously written from the heart. I spent many hours deciphering as I typed it for her. I left some of her misspelled words. Here is the beginning of her story:

THE LOST LOVE OF A CHILD: A TRUE STORY

When I was born I was fat. I was so pretty. My mother use to give me a party every night. I still can remember. I was only one year of age. When I was two I had the seizure. I use to do things I never thought I could do. I use to hit people with bottles. This is what my grandmother told me. I can't remember all of it but I can remember some. When I went to school they wanted to put me in a special school but my grandmother did not let them. They thought I was crazy, but I was not. I just was slow. But one time I got in a fight. I almost killed the girl. I was just that mad. So I went into a seizure. Everybody thought I was crazy. But later they understood that I am not. So later my seizure got worst. I had to take 500 phenobarbital three times a day. Everyone thought I was dead but I was not. But sometime it got just that bad. I thought I was dead too. But then I started to believe in God and when I did I got better and better. My grandmother use to allways pray for me and God heel me. I never had another seizure. My mother died when I was only two

Teachah Don't Know Nothin'

and a helf year old. When my mother died all I can remember is that she was running behind a tree with a knife and I saw blood on her dress. My grandmother said that my daddy sit up there and watch her died but my daddy thought she was sleeping. He said if she would had got to the doctor quik she would had lived. My daddy love my mother so much and still do. When they use to argue my daddy use to walk out of the door and be gone for two or three hour because she use to allway try to fight him. My aunt use to allway come over just to see a fight, but when my mother funeral came my daddy gave $300 to help for the funeral. Everybody sent some. I was a little girl. My daddy gave me and my sister money. He kept us with all kind of nice clothes. He really took good care of me and my sister but later I knew that I had to get over my mother died, so I did. Then I started live with my grandmother. Her and my daddy use to argue about me. My grandmother said to my daddy, 'Her mouth is too smart to me. I desirved more respect then that.' We use to argue old stuff. She said I think Im too pretty. I never really thought that but I never thought I was ugly, but we use to allso argue about my dad not give her a lot of money. So one time she say he has to quit come over. So I start to cry. I did not want my dad to go. I love him to much. I know my dad did not do enought for me and my sister but my grandmother want some of my dad money to.

Chapter Twelve

The ending of Darlene's story sounded hopeful. She said she was waiting until she was 18 so she could marry her boyfriend and get her twins out of foster care.

One day she asked me what "borderline" meant. She'd had a test to see if she could get her twins back and they told her she was "borderline." She brought me a copy of the test results showing her I.Q. scores. I explained to her that she scored lower on the test than some people, which meant she would have to work harder to learn things that others could learn more easily. She had severe visual problems, many emotional problems, and had not attended school regularly, any one of which would have caused her to make low scores on tests.

After she left the Bartelme Agency, she continued to send me updates on her story. I sent her paper, pens, and stamped envelopes. After her husband went to prison, she used the stamped envelopes to write to him. She recently called me in North Carolina when she got my number from Mrs. Dechter. She and her husband are living in a rented house, her husband is working in construction, and she has two children. She never got custody of her twins, but she said the girl had been to see her.

During English class, Hope, a quiet black girl who wore her hair neatly braided, wrote the following for one of her writing assignments:

> I use to be a runaway for all my years of life.
> But it didn't prove a thing, to try to run and sing,
> "Free at last, thank god almighty I'm Free at last."
> Only reason I ran because of my terrible past.
> I started running at seven,

Teachah Don't Know Nothin'

Thought I was so bad I won't go to heaven.
Ran away when I was eight, came back,
She said, "I'm going to put you in the state."
I ran when I was nine, my mother said,
"You committed a crime."
When I was ten she said I committed a sin.
I ran when I was eleven, she said
"You will never make it to heaven."
I ran away when I was twelve years old,
My dear sweet mother packed my clothes.
You can learn from this story, never run away
Because it really doesn't pay.
You should stop and think
Do you want to float or sink?

Though her name was Hope, she used the words float or sink. She - as well as most of the Bartelme girls and most of the kids at the other schools - did not see many alternatives in life. She figured she could just get by, as she'd been doing, or end her life. She did not think of swimming to get ahead.

When Vanessa Looney first came to Bartelme she seemed to be one of the more unstable girls I'd encountered. She was a slim, tall, angry, black girl. She grabbed things away from people, ran, and would not give them back. She tore up valuable papers, broke things that were valuable to others, and generally acted hostile and belligerent. She was living up to her name.

The first day in English class she said, "I don't like English. I'm not going to work in any book you give me."

Chapter Twelve

I said, "You don't have to, Vanessa. I have something else you can do that will give you an A in English." That got her attention. "If you write a page a day in this class, and don't cause any problems, you can get an A." I gave her a list of topics to use as ideas for writing, and told her she could choose any subject of interest. The only stipulation was that she had to complete a full page.

"I said, I ain't doin' no work," she snapped.

I gave her a folder with her name on it and a booklet with writing paper inside, then passed out folders to the other students. As the others began working, she opened her folder, read over the list of topics and asked, "Can I write about anything? What about stuff not on this list?"

"The list is to give you ideas," I said. "You may write about anything."

Her first day's writing was titled, "The World's Best Family," presenting a picture of her family that would make you think she came from a perfect family. I wrote a big A on the top corner of the paper, amazed that she deserved it. She had used almost perfect grammar and sentence structure, with excellent spelling.

Her next topic was "Death." She wrote about how much she was afraid of death and what happens after death and whether someone could come back and hurt you after they die. Her grandmother, who had been mean to her, had died recently. Vanessa was afraid her grandmother's ghost would come back and hurt her again. She usually wrote for the whole period and almost never stopped with one page.

When her writing folder became full, I gave her a binder with a clear plastic cover. She made a title page and

Teachah Don't Know Nothin'

decorated it and began to add some art to her writing. She wanted to take the binder home and show it to her boyfriend, Speedy. I'd made a rule that writing booklets could not go home until the end of the semester. It seemed so important to her that I made a copy so she could take the copy home.

She'd written so much about her personal problems that I asked her if I could show her book to Mrs. Stone, the counselor. Vanessa grinned and said proudly, "I'll take it to her." She was no longer a discipline problem. The few days when she said she wasn't in a mood to write, I told her she could do her writing in study hall, and she did. At the end of the grading period I gave her a certificate for "Excellence in Creative Writing."

As she was leaving for Christmas vacation, she said, "Mrs. Oglesby, I think you love me." I felt like that was one of the greatest compliments that had ever come my way. Many children over the years had said they loved me, but this was different. Vanessa had picked up on the fact that I cared about her.

There were few violent incidents in my classroom. One day Mr. Catania, the head teacher, was sitting near me in the lunchroom during my prep period when he nodded at a nearby class, "Just look, Mr. Geraci's kids are all out of control. His rules are too strict, so the girls rebel. In your classes the girls are well behaved because you don't have enough rules."

Chapter Twelve

I thought to myself, if I didn't have rules there would be as much chaos in my class as if I had rules that were too strict. His remark caused me to remember a discussion between the girls about what they thought would upset me.

Trina said, "Getting in her desk."

Lizette added, "Opening the file cabinet without permission."

Trina grinned, "Slapping her in the face."

Lizette laughed as she replied, "Oh no, she don't get upset about big stuff!"

I worked out a daily chart on which I kept a record of each student's effort, achievement, attitude, and behavior. Many times, when a student was doing something out of line, I only had to pull out the chart and the misbehavior stopped.

I was thankful for that chart when Jill came in very angry the morning after report cards came out. "What is this? I got A's on all my papers, and a C on my report card?"

"Well," I said, as I pulled out the chart, "it doesn't seem appropriate for me to give an A to a student who swears and calls the teacher a bitch for the first fifteen minutes of every class."

"Oh," she said, looking surprised, "A for work, and F for mouth makes a C."

Lizette wasn't as easy to appease. She came in yelling, "Bettah change that fuckin' F or I'll change it. You can't give me no F! I'm gonna slap your wisdom teeth in the back of your eyes so you can see all 43 of your teeth. You make my ass hurt - and I don't like no damn C! Next time you better give me a damn A."

137

Teachah Don't Know Nothin'

Still screaming, she left the room. I thought of Lizette as cute, for she was, until she opened her mouth. I disliked giving grades, especially failing grades, but if anybody deserved an F, Lizette did. She had done almost no schoolwork, and frequently was the cause of chaos in class.

One semester I volunteered to teach art the last two hours of the day. We had no art class and thought it would be good for the girls. It was. They loved it. One of the most talented of the art students, a tall blonde with blue eyes named Joanne, wanted to spend the whole afternoon in art instead of going to algebra one period. She wrote a note to Mr. Catania.

Dear Mr. Catania,

I am writing you on the subject of algerbra I can not do it because I took acid and it fryed the part of my brain cells to figure out algerbra. It is impossible for these brain cells to live again. I can only do art.

Love and kisses, Joanne

Her note didn't work; she remained in algebra. Joanne showed a great deal of artistic ability, but behavior problems kept her from achieving anything significant. I could see her potential for a career as a graphic artist and wished she could receive enough counseling to help her work through her anger and hostility.

Mr. Catania had another problem to deal with as a result of the art class. The girls were crocheting all over the school. In the art class at Simpson crocheting had been a big hit, so I tried it at Bartelme. Many of the girls carried

Chapter Twelve

their crocheting around with them and crocheted all during the day. Some of them were pregnant and were making baby clothes. Mr. Catania finally set rules about when they could crochet: during art, lunch, and morning break only.

The next year a donor gave enough typewriters to the school for a typing class, but we had no qualified teacher. I volunteered. I'd had typing in high school and did type a little, so thought I could help beginners learn what they needed for a start in typing.

While the students practiced their typing one morning, I stood in the doorway and saw one of my typing students go into another classroom and let loose with a barrage of swearing. In a few minutes she brushed past me, plopped down in her seat, pulled out some curlers and began putting them in her hair. She screamed, "I'm putting curlers in my hair and you can't stop me. Just try! I'm gonna kill you." I knew she was angry and needed to spout off, so I let her.

After she got her hair curled, she began typing. When she couldn't get the margins set she began screaming again. "I'm leavin' now! I'm gonna kill you!" She stomped out of the room, still yelling.

Barbara, a very pretty Hispanic girl with thick naturally curly hair who was sitting at the back of the room, also became frustrated with typing. She stopped her work, started twisting strands of her long hair, and muttered under her breath. From my desk, I asked, "Barbara, do you need help?"

She leaned forward and yelled, "Help? You can't tell me nothin'! You don't know nothin'! Your mother ever kick you out of your house?"

Teachah Don't Know Nothin'

"No, " I answered.
"You ever been on drugs?"
"No."
"You ever been hungry and ain't got nothin' to eat?"
"No."
"You ever been in jail?"
"No."
"You ever seen anybody killed?"
"No."
"You have a baby when you was fourteen?"
"No."
"See, I told you, you don't know nothin'!"

I knew Barbara was right. I didn't know nothin' about the kind of life she and the other girls had lived. I could never understand what they had lived through, nor ever really know how they felt, as often I tried to imagine myself walking in their shoes.

Chapter Thirteen

When a Bartelme girl reached eighteen, she was transferred to the Independent Living Program. That meant she moved from the group home into an apartment of her own, provided by the state. The state also paid her living expenses and gave her assistance with finding a job and learning to support herself.

Penny, the girl I kicked out of class, and the one who seemed particularly ungrateful for the help she received, got her own apartment. She received further help from one of the teachers at Bartelme, an outgoing teacher named Janet. Janet couldn't resist getting involved in the girls' lives. She often brought clothes and gifts to school for them, invited them to her home, paid them to clean her house, or helped them find work in homes of her friends. She found work for Penny as a babysitter for one of her neighbors.

Teachah Don't Know Nothin'

One week Penny didn't show up at Janet's home, where she was a frequent visitor, or for her babysitting job. Janet sent her son's girlfriend to check on Penny. Penny was dead. Her nude body had been stabbed many times. She had been dead for days. I heard two versions of what had happened. One said that several of the Bartelme girls had wanted to stay with Penny in her apartment, and killed her because she wouldn't let them. The other version involved drugs or prostitution.

Three of the girls from Bartelme were arrested for her murder and sent to Audy. A new student, who'd been in Audy, told me she heard one of them bragging about how they killed Penny.

Just months before she was murdered, Penny wrote this poem.

> TIME PASSED BY
> Time passed by
> Through the day and night
> Weekends sitting by
> Getting high
> Music playing
> People having a good time
> And time still
> Passing by
> The job of our life is
> Enjoying time
> Not just to let it
> Pass by

Though Penny was no longer a student at Bartelme, most of the girls knew her, so we held a memorial service for

Chapter Thirteen

her. Hers was not the only memorial we held that year. An exceptionally pretty girl with red hair and freckles named Lari was also killed - stabbed in the neck and hit with a blunt instrument, the paper said. She also had left the agency and was living with her boyfriend. Sometime later another former student's decomposed body was found in the canal. Rumor was that her pimp had done it.

Reports of these deaths did not help the Bartelme Agency's reputation. Neither did news that a prostitution ring functioned from one of the houses. For a while there was so much bad press that the Department of Children and Family Services stopped sending girls to Bartelme. The staff cared about and wanted to help the girls, but so many of them were severely troubled, and most were constantly in dangerous situations, that social workers and counselors had an almost impossible job.

For a few days I worked at another school for Bartelme Agency students, and while there I got Angie's story. I updated assignments on the board and went to the desk. Angie was seated near my desk and as soon as I sat down she began talking. "You came here to see we don't go off today?"

I knew what 'go off' meant, so I braced myself for a tough day.

After the other students were busy working, Angie pulled her chair closer to the desk and said, "I need to see a psychiatrist. That's what they told me. My probation officer won't come because she know I hold everything inside and then I explode and she knowed I'd explode. I don't talk to

Teachah Don't Know Nothin'

nobody. I just keep it all inside. I really need somebody to talk to."

Angie was unkempt, extremely fidgety and restless. She kept tracing a scar on her cheek as she talked, and rocked sideways, back and forth. I had the feeling she might go off, so I let her talk. For the next hour she talked and rocked, non-stop.

"Yesterday when them girls started fighting," she said, "and that girl put her hand in my face, I can't stand that. I didn't even hit her 'cause I'm on my last chance. I knowed I didn't have no more chances and I couldn't get in no more fights so I thought what to do and I just passed out.

"These girls here act so crazy they make me feel crazy. The police took Yolanda and Charlene. Tina was holdin' Latonya. Latonya was screamin' that she was gonna git 'em.

"You know, probation officers only give you three chances, and I don't get no more. She already give me six, and seven means I go to jail. Last night I was on the bed and I thought, 'Kill yo sef, Angie. Kill yo sef, Angie.' That's all I thought about. I was gonna put on my shoes and grab my purse and walk out in front of a car. Then Miss Wilkins talked to me and straightened out my head a little bit."

I wondered why she intended to grab her purse if she planned to kill herself. She kept rubbing the scar on her cheek and talking, still swaying from side to side.

"First chance I got was when I was on the bus and that girl put her hand in my face, and I can't stand that. I slapped her, and she did it again. I got all her stuff and when she got off the bus I got off with her. You know them rails over the

Chapter Thirteen

expressway? Well, I tried to throw her over, but the bus driver got off the bus and stopped me. Then I kicked and hit him, and he pressed charges.

"My step-father was messin' with me and I told my mother. She was goin' to kill him. She had the knives and gun and stuff on the table waitin', but she was shakin'. She just couldn't do it. When he started hittin' my little brother I just picked up the gun and pulled the trigger. One bullet went in the wall and one bullet went in his leg."

I wished I knew real short hand, and wrote as fast as I could, tying to get it all down. Don't think I miss much. My writing didn't seem to affect her for she kept talking.

"They let me off for that, so my real father killed him. When the police came to get him I hit 'em and kicked 'em and they throwed me in the car with my father. I said, 'OK, take us both.' They brought me back home and my father stayed there for three weeks. It was self-defense.

"Then, the next thing, this little boy at my house said, 'You black ugly big lips.' I didn't pay no attention. Then he got mad and threw a rock that hit my leg. I walked on up the steps. Then a big rock hit my back and I said, 'That's it!' and I turned and ran back down them steps and beat him up. His mother came out and started throwing Jiffy Mix boxes at me. Full Jiffy Mix boxes! I had Jiffy Mix marks all over my face. She came on up the steps and in my house after me. I didn't know what to do so I just picked up a knife and stuck her in the stomach.

"My brother has a big hole in his heart and he can't take no stress. One time my auntie was mad. She had bought a whole Family Pack of fish, Buffalo fish. My little sister was

145

Teachah Don't Know Nothin'

bad so my auntie ate all her fish and then she was tryin' to stuff food in her little boy, only one year old, pushin' the spoon down his throat, tryin' to make him eat. My brother ran out, 'cause he can't take stress. He'll die next time he passes out. So I picked up a chair and hit her with it.

"I saw my little sister get killed by a truck. It mashed her between the truck and another car. I was all dressed up, walkin' out with leathers and everything. I was always helpin' her fight and lyin' for her to keep her out of trouble.

"My daddy always gave me $100 or $150 a week. I gave part of it to my mother for food. We stayed in the projects and sometimes we ran out of food. I bought things for all my family. My father got a lot of kids. Half of them stay with their mothers. I don't know how many kids he got."

The teacher-aide stepped into the room to ask what I wanted to order for lunch. As soon as she left, Angie started up her monologue again. I listened, not sure I believed all of those experiences could belong to one teenage girl.

"Me and my mother don't get along. She try. I'm the problem. I want to do this and that, and she won't let me.

"Ain't nothin' in the streets, just rapists and killers. I know now. I wish I had a' listened. My mother told me about gettin' pregnant. The man don't suffer, you do. Life is really hard when you don't listen to your mother.

"I even tried to commit suicide a couple of times. My grandmother said, 'Don't never try to kill yosef. When the Lord wants you, he come and git you.' That woman taught me a lot. I wish she was still alive. If she was, my uncle

Chapter Thirteen

wouldn't be in jail and my auntie wouldn't be dead from cocaine.

"My uncle's wife's mother and father got sugar diabetes. Everybody in our family got sugar diabetes. My uncle died. He got hit by a truck tryin' to save our dog. The dog got away, but he got hit. My other uncle got hit by a train tryin' to save a cat.

"One time we was on the bus and this girl was gittin' on. We told her not to get on or we'd take her stuff. We wanted it and we took it. Alvira took a pen and hit her in the head. She had on a Liz Claiborne jacket and shoes, and a Coach bag, and you know them cost money. And then we seen her chains! Ain't no way she was gonna git away with them."

One of the other girls brought her math book to the desk, needing help with a problem. Angie kept rocking while I helped her. Then Angie continued to talk.

"My four-year-old brother had a stroke. One day my mother said, 'Willie, come here,' and he didn't. And she said, 'Willie, I said come here.' He said, 'I can't.' And he couldn't. Now his foot drag.

"My baby sister got third degree burns from her neck to her thighs. My mother put a pot on the stove to boil and my sister pulled a chair to the stove and pulled it all over her. She was in the hospital three months.

"My nine-year-old brother saw his stepfather stickin' tooth brushes up his little sister's vagina. Every time he saw his stepfather stick tooth brushes up his sisters he got mad, so he ran away. Men shouldn't go in they pants when they ain't got no business in they pants.

Teachah Don't Know Nothin'

"One time they took me to see a psychiatrist. I started playin' with my lips and actin' funny, acted like I was playin' a guitar. They thought I was crazy. It was funny.

"I hope my baby don't be like me when she grow up. My mother threw up her hands and gave me to the Lord. The Lord sho havin' fun punishin' me.

"Life is hard. I wish I could start over."

Then she asked me how old I was. When I told her, she was thoughtful for a moment, and said, "Well, I guess some people can have a hard life and come out soft."

With the kind of environment Angie lived in, I could understand how she could be so troubled. Most of the girls came from homes and areas of the city that caused problems for them, but Sherry came from what seemed an ideal environment. Her family lived in the upscale village of River Forest. Her mother was a teacher and her father an airline pilot, yet she was heavy into drugs, a very troubled girl. She was short and dumpy with dishwater-blond hair and a round face.

One morning she came in with a new watch. When I commented on it she told me how she got it. She and her boyfriend were out of money and she decided to make some. As she stood on the corner, a man stopped his car and she got in. As they were driving down Lake Shore Drive, she asked how much money he had and he told her. She said, "That's not enough. Take me back. I'm a minor and you'll get in trouble."

The man drove her back to Wilson Street, where he had picked her up. Her boyfriend was waiting and got in the

Chapter Thirteen

car. They made the man drive them to Belmont Park along the lake, beat him up, and took his watch and his money.

Sherry often came to school when it was obvious she was on some kind of drug. During a school picnic in a forest preserve, Mr. Catania discovered that she had left the group and joined some guys who were drinking beer and smoking marijuana.

One day in class we talked about our greatest fears. Sherry said her greatest fear was that she would end up as a bum on Wilson Street. I thought the place for bums in Chicago was Madison Street, so I drove down Wilson on the way home that day. I could see what she meant. The area had many halfway houses and homes for indigent people, many of whom were walking the street.

Some time later I visited a church on the corner of Wilson and Sheridan Road. After the service, refreshments were served in the church basement. About twenty or more people from the neighborhood came in to get food. The woman in charge fed the neighborhood visitors in a separate area from the regular church members. She said they came every Sunday. I thought of Sherry's fear of becoming a bum on Wilson and hoped some miracle would happen to prevent such a future for her.

Fear, to the Bartelme girls, was about more than the distant-future variety. They lived every day with fears of all varieties, and felt no sense of security that they would make it to the next day without catastrophe striking them or

Teachah Don't Know Nothin'

someone close by. Sherry wrote the following about another of her fears.

I fear when God comes back because I know if He comes back now I am going to hell and burn forever. A lot of people don't think that God is coming back but he is and the Bible says he will be back. But when he comes he is coming like a thief in the night, unexpectedly. When God comes back he is going to take all his people, the ones that are living right and serving God. The ones that don't go to heaven will be here to face tribulation, and tribulation is nothing like heaven. God is going to let the devil's people take over for about nine months and they are going to terrorize people something terrible.

Chapter Fourteen

One day I asked the girls in English class if they'd ever known anybody who got killed. Silly question. I just couldn't make myself comprehend that killing was so much a part of life for the girls.

Vanessa's brother was shot at the mailbox on New Year's Eve when people were shooting just for the fun of it. Trinetta's girlfriend was killed in a car accident, and her boyfriend was found stabbed to death on July 4th. Angel's brother was killed by John Gacy (the mass murderer). Her boyfriend was killed by drug dealers, he was making $1,000 a week and they thought that was too much, so they shot him and threw him in the river. Nancy remembered Tom who "got shot in the head three times."

They talked about the killings as they would have anything else, with almost no emotion. I felt as though a

Teachah Don't Know Nothin'

big black cloud were hanging over me for some time after listening to that discussion. Not only had I never seen anyone get killed, I'd never known anyone who had been killed. These kids surely had to wrap some kind of armor around them just to make it through the day.

All along, at the other schools too, there had been some talk among the students about street gangs. I knew very little about street gangs and had only a cursory interest. The *Chicago Tribune* ran a series of articles about gangs and I made copies for the girls and one for the bulletin board. Mr. Catania took one look at the bulletin board and said, "That comes down. Nothing related to gangs can be allowed in the school."

I thought since the articles were published in the *Tribune* they would be suitable for study in class. I had no idea how much gangs were a part of life for many of the girls. Barbara, the typing student who told me I didn't know nothin', called herself a Latin Queen. She told the following story.

"My father was a big man in the Latin Kings. He was killed a year ago. I have been in gangs all my life, and my father took me with him wherever he went. I liked being a part of the gang. It was a great way to live.

"A man who hated my father snitched on my father, set his ass up. My father went to Puerto Rico to get coke and pot, and got really good stuff. People came to my father instead of that man, and he said my father took away his

Chapter Fourteen

business. My father never gave people bullshit like flour instead of the real stuff, like that man did.

"That man went to the police station and told the police and they came to our house. My father thought they were coming because of the gangs, and they came in and found shit all over the house. They put my father in jail and I had to go back and live with my mother. When my father got out he took care of that motherfucker.

"I went to visit my sister who lived two blocks into the Gangsters' territory, and when I rang the doorbell I felt someone pull back on my hair and they really gave it to me. I was pregnant. I lived, but it killed my baby. Then the police took me and put me in the Audy Home.

"In the summer when it's hot in Humbolt Park, every day there's fights. Then it's really going on.

"I had a friend who couldn't hear or speak. He used sign language. He gave us them little books of sign language. He was so sweet. He used to love little kids and played with the little kids.

"In sign language the sign for peace and love was a gang sign, and the people told him to use it. He made the sign for peace and love, and they stabbed him and beat him and killed him. Everybody who knew him pitched in $100 to help bury him. They really killed him bad. My brother got out his gun to kill them but they left before he got there.

"After my father was killed it was my place to fill in for him. Now I have his job to do and I am next on the Gangsters' hit list. I've seen lots of people killed when I went everywhere with my father. Killing is no big deal. Everybody does it.

Teachah Don't Know Nothin'

"My father told the gang to watch out for me and keep me from doing anything bad. I had to take over from my father to show respect for him. I used to like to fight and gang bang. I was real bad. Now that I've been away for six months, I'm different. I see it's not the only way of life. I used to think it was all of life, and I liked it. "

Barbara said most of the information in the newspaper article about gangs was correct, but that a lot was left out. As she and Trinetta were taking the newspaper article from the bulletin board, she said to Trinetta, "Gang bangers would really love Mrs. Oglesby."

Her use of 'gang bangers' carried no sexual connotation. I had learned enough of the terms the kids used to know that she simply meant gang activities, and I understood her remark about me to mean that I was willing to listen to people who were in gangs talk without judging. I was more than willing to listen because I wanted to learn about the gangs and everything in the world of these kids.

The kids used some common words in unusual ways, a practice that often made for misunderstandings. One example is the case of Kitty, a tiny little blond originally from Kentucky. She said, "When I first came here, somebody asked me, 'What do you ride?' And I said, 'A horse,' and they almost killed me. You don't joke about your gang. I didn't know they were asking me what was my gang."

I gradually compiled a list of the terms the kids used. And I often pulled out a tape recorder to capture what they were saying. All the kids loved to have the tape player running while they talked and liked to listen to the tape

Chapter Fourteen

later. In the art class at Bartelme, while the girls were crocheting, I recorded their conversation. They were upset because a new student had said every girl in Bartelme was a bitch. Toward the end of the conversation they spoke of gangs, mentioning the two Chicago gangs, the Vice Lords (also referred to as People) and Gangster Disciples (called Folks). Here's the taped conversation:

Darlene: "They ain't nobody a bitch. I kept my child. And I might be a little bit slow on readin' and shit, but I ain't no hoe. I'm tryin' to catch up wid it. She thinking she too cute and shit. She look like a hoe with all that make-up and stuff on. She don't even know me."

Myself: "She wasn't talking about you girls, was she?"

Darlene: "She say everybody in this school is a bitch. And she say, 'specially Chase House. She de only bitch dare. She's every name in the motherfucking book. She put her baby up for adoption."

Myself: "What's putting her baby up for adoption got to do with anything?"

Darlene: "We don't care about dat. Dat's up to her conscious. She shouldn't call nobody a bitch, 'cause she the only bitch in here. She de only female dog. The only female dog. The lowest dog in the whole wide world. Her mother have to tie a poke chop around her neck to even git a dog to come close to her."

Myself: "She's surely a cute girl."

Lizette: "Like a she dog, you mean."

Darlene: "If I comb my hair, and take off my glasses, I'll run rings around her. Don't let me get started."

Lizette: "She's stupid, though. She think she too cute."

Teachah Don't Know Nothin'

Darlene: "I'm gonna tell her, 'I don't appreciate you callin' me a bitch.' Then I'm just gonna go on about my business. I didn't do nothin' to her."

Lizette: "Hell, didn't nobody do nothin' to her."

Darlene: "Just 'cause she put her kid up for adoption she takin' it out on all o' us. It ain't our fault."

Lizette: "She shouldn't a been too fast to drop her pants if she don't want a baby."

Betty: "It'll be a cold day in hell before I let her call me a bitch."

Lizette: "I can fight, goddamnit. I'll rip her little ass off. Once I git pissed off, ain't nothin gonna stop me."

Betty: "Ain't nobody in here worth you goin to Audy."

Lizette: "She the only four-leg bitch in here, and say woof woof."

Betty: "Darlene, what gang you in? Big G?"

Lizette: "Did you see 'bout the girls' gangs on the news last night?"

Darlene: "I'm a nice person, but somebody always keep pushin' me to the edge, I would really have to do something to put them in check."

Betty: "Why? Cause you a Gangster, right?"

Darlene: "I'm serious. I don't git this mad unless you push me. And she pushed me, 'cause I don't appreciate nobody callin' me no bitch. My mama had me. I came out with two legs, not four. She came out with four."

Betty: "You goin off, Darlene?"

Darlene: "'Cause she makin' me mad."

Chapter Fourteen

Cheryl: "I called her a bitch today. Didn't you hear me? I said, I ain't got time for no lil' fifteen-year-old bitch. She didn't say nothin'."

Darlene: "She think I'm scared o' her. We'll let her know she can't whup no butts here. I'll spit on her and think nothin' of it."

Darlene: "How old is you, Mrs. Oglesby?"

Cheryl: "Fifty-seven. Old lady. Goin' on sixty. But don't she look good to be so old?"

Betty: "I hit Reo, didn't I?"

Darlene: "She jist dress like that for fun."

Betty: "She nice though. I bet she a big G."

Cheryl: "I'm a Vice Lord. I'm gonna whup yo ass."

Betty: "Oh, you a VL."

Toy Lee: "You can be People, Vice Lord, or whoever you wanta be. I'm Toy Lee and I can whup yo ass."

Betty: "Now, one Folks can call another Folks a bitch. But better no People call me a bitch."

Darlene: "Yeah, you don't fight you own Folks."

Betty: "Yeah, you git a violation for that. Lizette's sister was gonna git in a fight, but we had to talk it out 'cause we both Disciples and we can't fight each other. We s'posed to stick together, not apart. If she was callin' Folks names, I'd git up and steal on her. (hit her.) I know I would. Don't care who around. Straight up. That's why me and that chick Claudette didn't git along. She said she VL and I said I be GD. There was 3 VL's in the house and one Folks, that be me. I said, straight up, I'm tall Folks, you dig? I said I ain't gonna throw down my nation for nobody."

157

Teachah Don't Know Nothin'

In their conversation the girls mentioned Reo, one of the most memorable of the Bartelme students - a white girl who dressed to be noticed. Once you saw her you didn't forget her. She said she was dressing like Madonna - with odd clothing and hairstyles, often with draped wraps and unmatched boots or shoes. And unusual jewelry, too, of course, as well as ribbons and scarves, and hair dye and face paint. Every day's outfit differed from the one before.

Reo said she had been born with a "gift." She meant she was psychic, and she read the girls' palms. I thought she did have some psychic ability, and thought she might in the future earn her living as a psychic. I wanted to help her learn astrology, but the social workers wouldn't allow it. Instead she, like most of the girls, with no wage-earning skill, got pregnant several times and ended up living on welfare. No follow-up was done with the girls but often we either saw them on the streets or heard rumors about them.

I never ceased being moved by the stories I heard from them. Once, during the last period of the day, three girls were sitting around a table near my desk talking about why they had tried to kill themselves. They were not aware I was listening.

Trina said she had been beaten with wet extension cords, and hit with bats, and once was pushed from a second floor window by her mother. When she took so many pills she passed out in math class, her mother was called to school and the police came there to pick up the mother. She tried to hit Trina even while they were in the school office.

Melinda said her father physically and sexually abused the four children in the family. She was the second

Chapter Fourteen

daughter. When her father beat them, and they moved, he continued to beat until they didn't move. Her other sisters could take it without moving, but Melinda couldn't. Sometimes she ran and if she got under the bed, he "picked up the whole damn bed" to get to her. He used extension cords, often putting her in the bathtub so the blows would be more painful because she was wet. She said he made them sit at the table all night, wouldn't let them sleep. If they nodded he would hit them, or take them to the bathroom and stick their heads in the toilet after he had urinated in it. He also burned them with a hot iron. She said she took pills to kill herself more than once, then lay down on the bed, thinking she wouldn't wake up again, but every time her eyes opened and she lived.

Glenda said her mother held her head between her legs while she beat her with an extension cord.

They talked seriously, quietly, not noticing that I was there. Most of the time I could leave school at school - forget the job when I left for the day - but that day, tears rolled down my cheeks as I drove home.

How could I remain detached and objective? Over and over I told myself to leave it at school. If I became involved emotionally with the problems of these girls I'd never be able to function as a teacher. I could understand their anger and hostility toward the world, and their outbursts at everyone. So often I asked myself what I could do to help, and felt helpless. I could help them succeed a little in school. I could listen. I could accept them as they were, but the difficulties went so deep, with such a long history

Teachah Don't Know Nothin'

involved, that often I felt as hopeless for them as they felt about themselves.

When I thought of my own childhood and teen years, I thought I'd had it rough. My father was blind and my mother worked hard helping him to make enough for us to survive, leaving the care of three younger children and the housework to me. I'd thought I was robbed of a childhood because of so much responsibility and duty at such an early age. Compared with the childhood of these girls, mine was the Garden of Eden.

So many of the girls wrote about needing help, but didn't verbalize the need. Evidently it was easier for them to express their deepest feelings on paper than to talk about them. Lari, one of the girls who got murdered, wrote the following:

> As I sit at night and my thoughts are free flowing, I write how I feel. I have so much on my mind that I can't take it any more.
>
> Life was meant to be something special. Why do people treat you the way they do? People were put on earth as human beings, not animals! This isn't the planet of the apes. Why do people leave? I need somebody! Why won't anybody help me? I know what hurt is. Hurt is evil; it has no feelings.

Another Bartelme girl wrote the following poem. I wish I could remember her name.

MY WORDS

Whenever I am feeling down and up tight
I pick up my pen and begin to write.
Sometimes I haven't got much to say,

Chapter Fourteen

But it helps me to chase the clouds away.
My writing may not make sense to you,
What I'm saying may not be new.
I use my words as weapons to fight loneliness and fear,
When depression and pain come, my words dry my tears.
For those of you who have everything and don't need a thing,
You won't understand what I'm saying behind these walls.
You may think my poems sound silly and absurd
Though I can't imagine life without my words.
Writing my messages isn't a pastime or a hobby or a game,
These words of mine keep me from going insane.
If the day ever comes that I can't write my words anymore
That will be the day I'll ask God to let me through His door.

Another girl who certainly needed help many times was Norma, a very plain drab girl of fourteen with braces on both upper and lower teeth who looked several years younger than she was. Her first composition began this way:

> When I was little I lived with my grandmother. My father tried to take me away from my grandmother. When I was nine years old my father raped me. He spent two years in jail and I spent a week in the hospital. If I ever see my father again I will kill him.

Teachah Don't Know Nothin'

Frequently the students (at Bartelme and other schools) expressed their thoughts on punishment. They had no use for it. They thought it didn't do any good at all, for anybody. Here's a paper by a soft-spoken blonde named Stephanie that expresses the opinion held by most of the students.

> Punishments really sucks to me. I don't understand why they have such things as punishments. They don't do any good to anyone. The only thing I see they do, are to make you want to do the crime over and over again. Just as Audy Home if you steal something and get caught the judge give you time upstairs. I don't understand why. Once you steal you are going to always steals. The same with whupins. If your parents whip you, that's not going to do anything but make you do the same thing over again. That's why I don't understand why they have this system called punishments. It doesn't help anyone do anything better.

This same opinion was held for sentences given by courts, and the kids also had a strong disrespect for law enforcement. Celeste wrote the following:

> 'We serve and protect.' As we all know, this is written on the side of police cars. It's my belief that this should be the opposite, for the simple reason that the police do the opposite.
>
> I feel that the police are assholes because I've had some bad experiences with them. For instance, one day there were some problems in Chase House and a fight started. The police arrived at the house to 'serve and protect.' One of the girls resisted arrest, so the police

Chapter Fourteen

started beating her, cursing her, and slapping her around. When I told them to stop, they arrested me. When we got in the car the police started hitting us because one of the girls was crying.

The police are also well known for busting people. Often the police will stop you for no reason. For example, if you walk down the street and drop something then pick it up, you are a likely suspect for drug dealing. They also stop you for drinking or smoking reefer. They confiscate it and get high themselves. A lot of times the police can be paid off. It just depends how much money you have.

In conclusion, I believe the police are prejudice and ignorant. I have never trusted them and never will.

All the girls at Bartelme were under seventeen. How could they concentrate enough to learn anything academic when such appalling stuff was going on in their personal lives?

Chapter Fifteen

The next fall when we were discussing what would be taught, Mr. Catania wanted to add three new classes to the curriculum: sewing, cooking, and a family living course that would focus on the basics of purchasing food and caring for a home. I volunteered to handle the new courses, none of which I had taught before, and no training for teaching them. I didn't know when I volunteered that the next decision would be that the cooking class - because it would be "the best way for them to learn to cook" - would be responsible for serving the daily meal at school.

Talk about too much to do! I had taken on an almost impossible task. Five to ten disturbed girls preparing a meal for forty people! We fed the students, teachers, and the Bartelme Agency staff. The meal had to be prepared in one hour. Every Thursday I went shopping after school. I must have been crazy when I agreed to do that, and my creative

Teachah Don't Know Nothin'

bent made more work for me, for I didn't always stick with simple menus. I chose unusual things like Chinese meals that included won tons and egg rolls, or other ethnic kinds of food.

The thing that bothered me most was the way the cooks were always licking their fingers and the spoons while they were cooking. I finally told them that no student would receive a passing grade if I saw her lick her fingers or lick a spoon while cooking. I could manage a little dinky kitchen, all the shopping, the cleanup, and making sure the girls washed their hands, but licking and continuing to work with food was too much!

We had to have everything cleaned up and ready for the next class by the end of the lunch period. After several months, Mr. Catania asked me why I didn't have the cleanup completed before time to start teaching art.

I said, "Why don't you try it?"

He did, for a week, but couldn't get the girls to help clean up any more than I could, and found himself doing it alone most of the time, as I had. After that week, he didn't help with cleanup any more, but he didn't complain any more, either.

During family living class, I taught the girls to write checks. I still had some personal checks from a closed account and used them to teach the girls how to write checks. I explained to them that the account was closed and the checks were no good, but within a few days a social worker called me over to the agency's office to tell me the girls had taken those checks, forged my signature, and cashed them.

Chapter Fifteen

When that year was over, I told Mr. Catania I wanted my old job back. No more teaching cooking, check writing, sewing, or art. I wanted to teach a regular classroom of English, Social Studies or Math. Thank goodness he agreed that I could do just that.

It was in my English class that I became aware of the powerful effect of the sound "anh." If, for example, a student started to open a drawer and I didn't want her to, I'd say "Anh," and she'd stop. If a fight were starting, I could often stop it with a stern "Anh!"

I think I'd always used the sound instinctively as I worked with kids, but in that class I became aware of the sound's effect, and got excited as I consciously used it and watched the reaction. Usually the undesired behavior was interrupted, and neither the student nor I made any other comment.

Sure gave me a great feeling when it stopped fights. Most of the time we teachers didn't know what a fight was about, probably some stupid thing, like "She looked at me like that." One student touching another, or picking up another's pencil, might provoke violence.

Once I got between two girls who were beginning a fight in class and said, "Now, if you want to fight, you need a referee. Go ask Mr. Catania to watch and see who wins the fight." They both laughed and sat down.

Fights were not unusual, but for three or more girls to be involved was unusual. One day a brawl broke out in the lunchroom - a major upheaval. The teacher-aide named Alberta, a small black woman who liked to control everything, got right in the middle of it. She jumped up and

Teachah Don't Know Nothin'

down and yelled, "I will not have this! I will not have this!" If the other teachers and I had not been busy grabbing girls to stop the fight, we would have sat back and laughed at Alberta. She jumped and yelled, and the girls fought their way around her.

One time when Mr. Catania was away and I was in charge, Darlene and Michelle came running out of second period class. Darlene said, "That teacher is child-molesting Michelle."

"Tell me what happened."

Darlene did the talking. "He asked Michelle to sit in a chair close to him, and then he asked her a personal question."

"What kind of a personal question?"

"He said he wanted us to be his girlfriends. I'm going to the police and report this. He's contributing to the delinquency of a minor."

After a little investigation, I determined that the teacher had not said or done anything wrong. I said, "Darlene, he was not molesting anyone. He is a nice substitute teacher who wants you girls to like him."

The girls took off to a special program on sex education. I hoped they would forget the incident. They didn't. They complained to an agency social worker and she came over to talk with me about it. As Darlene left at the end of the day she said, "That man was very child-molesting, and if you don't do something I'm going to the police." I had no alternative but to report the incident to Mr. Hahn, the

Chapter Fifteen

principal of Audy and its branches. The substitute did not come back to our school.

Within a few weeks, the girls complained about another male teacher, Mr. Archie. The adults sided with Mr. Archie, sure he had done nothing wrong, but the laws were that any complaint relating to sex meant the teacher had to be removed. He and I had become good friends and I hated so much to see him leave, especially under the stigma of an unfounded accusation. Mr. Hahn gave him a job at another branch school, but the complaint would remain on his record.

When the girls tried wielding their power again, with a complaint against the physical education teacher, it didn't work. We had only recently become fortunate enough to have a physical education class, so somehow he was allowed to stay with us until the end of the school year. The next year we again had no physical education class.

We teachers were of the opinion that the girls had found a way to exercise power and were enjoying using it. We had only one male teacher left, and Mr. O'Connor had been there so long I suppose they were afraid to accuse him. So few men were able to work with the girls, though the girls certainly needed some decent men around.

Norma, the girl who intended to kill her father if she saw him again, came to class from seeing the social worker, threw her arms around me and cried, "Oh, Mrs. Oglesby, they think I'm a whore." When I asked what would cause them to think a thing like that, she said, "Just because those guys call me on the phone all the time and I don't know them."

Teachah Don't Know Nothin'

The following Monday Norma said she'd probably be leaving soon. Over the weekend, she said, she had been at the home of a girlfriend to listen to records and drink beer. The girl asked Norma to come in the bedroom to see something. Three guys were there, one very big man with a gun and lots of cameras and lights. They drugged her and kept her there for hours, having sex with her and taking pictures.

After she told the social workers, the men were picked up, released on bond, and were out to get Norma. Several other students were known to be involved in procuring girls for a porno ring. Of course, it made the newspapers, and was a strike against the agency.

One morning Rolanda, one of the girls reportedly involved with the porno ring, was showing the other girls a paper, and when I walked up she showed it to me. She had divided the paper into three columns. In one column she listed the date and time, the next she wrote who she had sex with, and on the right side, when her period started or didn't start. She explained: "The purpose of the paper is so I ain't gonna be like the rest of these girls. I'm gonna know who the father of my baby is."

I lost some of my respect for the foster home program while there. The girls had often been in many foster homes, and sometimes were mistreated there. Laura told me about the last foster home she was in. The mother worked on Saturdays and the father bought her special clothes and took her out to "work" that day, in Elgin. I was surprised that she could do prostitution in such a small town as Elgin.

Chapter Fifteen

The Bartelme Agency and its schools and group homes had their roots in a home for "wayward girls" begun in the 1920s in her own home by Mary Bartelme, Illinois's first woman judge. She said, "There are no bad children. There are confused, neglected, love-starved and resentful children, and what they need most I try to give them - understanding and a fresh start in the right direction."

Understanding and a fresh start in the right direction might have been what they needed when Mary Bartelme worked with wayward girls, but for the girls I taught at Bartelme for eight years, such a simple solution was a gross understatement.

Chapter Sixteen

Cook County Juvenile Temporary Detention Center School. The school is on the second floor - just above the courtroom, just below the jail of the juvenile court building, which is near the intersection of Roosevelt Road and Ogden Avenue on the near west side. The jail used to be called the Arthur J. Audy Children's Home, and many of its occupants still call it the Audy Home.

Some of the students are being tried as adults on charges of rape, murder, robbery, or assault. Many dropped out of school years ago. But once in jail, they have no choice - this is one school they must attend. There are classes in math, social studies, science, English, and art taught by a number of enterprising teachers, including Dee Oglesby.

Ben Joravsky, of Chicago's *Reader Newspaper*, wrote those words in an article about the school after I'd worked at the detention center for about a year.

Teachah Don't Know Nothin'

When we learned Bartelme School would be closed, I wrote Mr. Hahn a long letter. I listed my many qualifications for teaching at the detention center, including the calming effect I had on violent kids. I practically begged him to bring me to the Audy.

Not often did a job open at Audy because teachers usually stayed for years. Most were older teachers with many years of teaching behind them. They appreciated the twelve-month salary, as well as the lack of pressure toward academic progress with the students, and the fact that it was easy to dismiss a misbehaving student from class. (There was always a guard handy.)

Mr. Hahn created a place for me. He gave me a job as reading tutor. I used a corner of the library for my work. The library was used for assigning kids to classrooms, testing, and conferences with probation officers, attorneys, and social workers, but not as a library. From the achievement test lists, I chose two kids to work with during each period, who's reading scores were grades one and two.

The library had lots of books, none of them suitable for teaching reading. I pulled out a few books that weren't too difficult and contained pictures. We struggled with those books for a week or two while I became more and more frustrated. The students didn't complain. They were glad to get special attention. They struggled along, using markers under the words or pencils to point at words, but I did most of the reading.

One day I thought, well, if they can't read from these books, maybe they can write. I pulled out some lined paper

Chapter Sixteen

and pencils. "Today we'll try something different. Write a story and I'll help you spell the words you don't know."

The student asked, "What'll I write about?"

I hadn't thought that far ahead. "Tell me about something you like to do."

Mike was a cute little freckle-faced kid. He asked, "Can I write about my Blazer?" We wrote, "My Blazer is candy-apple red. . . ." I wrote most of the words on my paper for him to copy. When he was finished he could read it with a little help, to Randy, a tall brown-faced boy. We did that for a few days, and when Randy was struggling to read what he'd written, I wondered how much better he would be able to read it if the words were typed.

I told the boys I was going to type their stories that night. Mike said, "Type about my Blazer!" I typed each story double-spaced, with the title at top center and the student's name as author below the story.

Next day Mike picked up the stack of typed pages. "Where is it? Where is it? Oh, here it is! It's beautiful! Just look at it. It's the prettiest thing I've ever seen." Randy reached for it. " No!" Mike said, "Don't read it! Just *look* at it. That's about my Blazer. Now, I'll read it to you."

You'd have thought I'd given Mike his freedom, he was so happy.

At first I made only one copy and the kid took the copy, so we didn't have it to read later. I started making two copies. Soon even those copies were disappearing, but our stack of stories kept growing.

Teachah Don't Know Nothin'

Ever since I'd been working with the inner city students, I had paid attention to the slang the kids used. One day I realized I hadn't learned as much as I thought I had.

I witnessed a fight in the hallway, and Mr. Ray, the north side counselor, said, "You witnessed this, you'll have to write the incident report." I asked him what to say on it. "Just say he stole on him," he said.

"Stole on him? What does that mean?"

He looked at me as if I were stupid, shrugged his shoulders and said, "Just write it. Everybody knows what that means."

Everybody maybe, except me, so I asked the kids. They laughed, and looked at me as Mr. Ray had. "When you steal on somebody, you just walk up and hit him for no reason." I wrote the word on my desktop calendar, the kind where you flip a page a day. Routinely I jotted down notes on those pages. They became my file on the new language I was learning.

A third boy joined the sessions with Mike and Randy when Mr. Ray asked me to take him. Bubba was a seventeen-year-old being tried for a juvenile crime. He was extremely large, almost as big as two of the other kids. His story is called "How I Got Here":

> I've been in trouble ever since I was little. Robbery, and misdemeanor things like breaking into houses. But I was with somebody else when I broke into a crib. I've got a record since I was eleven years old. That was battery. I had a fight with a kid. My old man always

Chapter Sixteen

said if someone messes with you just pick up something and bust their head. So I did. I hit him with a bottle. The bottle broke and I busted his head. He went to the hospital. His old girl came to my crib and she was talking to my mother. She told my mother to pay for the hospital bills and leave it alone. My old girl paid and I didn't go to court. Ever since then I just like fighting.

I'm in a gang. That's what made me get into a gang, because I'm always fighting. Nothing you can do about it. I joined the gang for a lot of reasons.

1. My friends are in it.

2. You can always fight and get away with it, most of the time.

3. A lot of people know you. I got a reputation. If someone gets killed around the hood, the cops come to me. Anything that happens around the hood, the cops come to me. That's why I'm in here now, cause of my reputation in the neighborhood.

4. You get pistols. I got one. The 9millimeter automatic and the 12 Gage are the two I like the best of all my guns. I gave the .22 to my sister.

I got up in here this time for robbing a crib with my dogs, three pit bulls. Had one in front, one inside with me, and one in the back. I didn't rob her crib. She took me to court because I'm the only one with pit bulls. They protect me, my house, and my drugs. They do a lot of things, and people want to kill them. Now, that trips me out.

Teachah Don't Know Nothin'

    My first pit bull I got when I was eight. My cousin watched over it for me. I grew up with my pits. Me and my cousin trained them. They're trained to kill and protect. That's it. We trained them that, to attack people.

Randy didn't want to read his story aloud. Its title was, "Being Alone." Mike squinted his freckled face and said, "Everybody's always alone. I don't like to be alone."

Bubba, the big guy, said, "I know what he's talking about. The worst part is upstairs when they lock that door and you can't see nothin' but them brick walls. I'm really scared then."

Randy said, "When they put you in confinement and you can't see nobody and can't talk to nobody. Then you really by yourself and you really scared."

Mike grinned. "There's a brick loose in the room they put me in. I scratched till I got it out and me and the boy next to me talk all night."

I wanted to say something that would help them feel more comfortable about being alone. "We're all alone, most of the time. When I'm alone and feeling scared I talk to God. God's always with you."

Randy said, "I pray to God all the time. But that don't make me feel better."

I said, "I'm not talking about praying to a God in heaven. I mean talk to the God that's close to you, all around you all the time."

"Ain't never done that," Randy said.

Bubba asked me, "You mean you get scared, too? Are you scared of being alone?"

Chapter Sixteen

"Oh, yes, I get scared. Not so much now that I'm older. I like to be by myself a lot of the time now. But I'd probably be scared of being locked up in a room alone. Then I'd have to find some way of feeling not alone, and safe."

When the boys reached seventeen, they were transferred out of Audy unless they were being tried for juvenile crimes, as Bubba was. He stayed with me for many months, and after he left Mr. Ray came by a number of times, pleased about "what we did for Bubba."

Another boy in Bubba's category was Blacky, a seventeen-year-old Hispanic. His teacher told me he was a non-reader. He told me he learned to read by first writing his name, then drawing pictures and lines. I gave him a book of the stories written by the students. He said, "But I can't read." I told him I wanted to find out how much reading he knew. I read a list of titles until he decided on one. He could recognize only a few words, so I began reading a story with him, pointing to each word. When guns were mentioned, he started telling me about his guns and bullets, reached for a paper and pencil and began drawing pictures of his guns. He was more interested in drawing and talking than reading.

On the following day, I had copied his picture and typed the little he had written. He asked for colors, red and yellow, then painted flames under each gun. The picture he drew of a person's head represented himself. A six-pointed star above and some symbols were signs for his gang.

He then said he wanted to read about gangs. We chose a story titled, "When My Homey Got Shot." I read it to him while he followed along with me. As we completed the first

179

Teachah Don't Know Nothin'

story, he said, "Next." After the next one he again said, "Next." After the third story, he pointed to the first one and asked if I could make him a story like that. "The same thing happened to me," he said, "but one part is different."

He pulled up his prison shirt, revealing a wide surgical scar down the middle of his stomach and two round scars on each side. Pointing to the round scars, he said, "The bullet went in here, and came out here, and the doctor operated here, and he put in about two-hundred stitches."

He gave me instructions. "Change this to say 'Blacky,' and this to say 'wicky,' and take out this part and put in 'When me and him went to get some wicky, we was walking down the street and they shot us. They shot us behind the train station. They came out and shot six times and shot me beside my stomach.'" He asked me to make two copies, one for his mother, and then asked, "Got any more about gangs?" Here's the story he read.

WHEN MY HOMEY GOT SHOT

He was at my house. Me and him were eating pizza and he said, "Let's get high." So I told him to go get the bow and my friend. He went to get the bow, and then I heard six shots. When I went over there he was laying on the tree. He was tied up to the tree and shot five times. One shot hit the tree. When I went over there I started to cry and untied him off the tree. Then the police got there and told me that I should of left him tied on the tree for they could take fingerprints. But I couldn't leave him tied on the tree cause it hurted me. It hurts to lose a friend. But then I went to the wake and he got buried the next day. Then I missed him a

Chapter Sixteen

lot. He was my best friend. When he died we went back for revenge, but nothing worked out. Then two months later the same guys who did it came by the neighborhood and the boys shot them up. I wasn't there but they told me. When I found out I was happy cause that's the way it is. They killed my homey so they got what they had coming. They knew they weren't going to get away with it. Someday they had to pay for what they did. We are Disciples and my nation misses him a lot. When we got revenge we threw a meeting and talked about it and the boys thought they did good. But those guys who got killed had friends too, and then they came back for revenge and tried to kill one of the boys. He was shot bad, but he made it. This will never stop. That's the way it is. They kill us and we kill them. It would just keep just like that, but as we get old it will stop maybe. So that's all about my nation. It's all about revenge.

Then he said he wanted to write a story, "cause my Folks need me back in my hood." As we finished the writing, he pointed to a typed story and asked, "You gonna write it up like this?"

MY FOLKS NEED ME BACK IN MY HOOD

My Folks need me back in my hood because they shot a couple of my Folks, Vicious Joe and Jose, and they wrote me, and my mother told me that they shot Joe. So while I'm locked up in the Audy Home, those boys that are not my boys are pulling hits on my boys, and my boys said, "We need you back in the hood, Blacky D., to pull our hits. You're the only one who

Teachah Don't Know Nothin'

can get away with it." I got a man in here that knows about the hits I pull. He knows how much rank I pull. So he goes around, makes moves, and finds out all about me. He comes to see me. I shot one of his good best friends. His name was Ralphie. Shot him right here in the neck and killed him. After I shot him, I got away from our hood for a while and my family moved to the north side. Since that day I shot him, I chilled out on gang-banging. That day I quit my organization. I'm the president. I quit. I'm not in a gang, but in this joint I'm a D, 'cause if you say you ain't nothin', it's worse for you in here.

Blacky said he really wanted to learn to read, and was beginning to read the Bible. "I prayed to God to help me to read. Then I read. It helped, too. I freaked out. A word I couldn't pronounce, it just came out! You see, everybody need some kind of God. You should make up your own God if you ain't got none. Last night in Bible study this picture flipped in my mind, a picture of the electric chair, with chains, and a man with horns."

He wrote a letter to his mother and printed in very large letters at the bottom of the page, "MY OWN WRITING MA," and spent nearly an hour drawing and coloring around those words with flowers and designs. He wrote on the back of the envelope, "Sealed with a kiss, cause a lick don't stick."

Working with students such as Blacky didn't frighten me, but I was intimidated by all the locked doors. One day during lunchtime I started for the office. I walked to the end of the hallway, turned the corner on the south side of the

Chapter Sixteen

building as I usually did, and found that the hallway ended about halfway down. The rooms and hall were deserted. I was sure there had been no wall there before, and started feeling uneasy. I walked back and down to get out on the north side. I discovered my key wouldn't fit the exit door on the north side. A teacher in a room nearby opened the door for me. I found myself in an enclosure with four doors. My keys fit none of them. Now I was frightened. Someone knocked on a little high window and pointed to a door. I heard a click and the door opened. "You need to knock so I know you're there and I can let you out," the guard said.

Returning from the office, I decided I would try to return my usual way, through the south side where the wall had stopped me before. My key fit the two doors leading to the school. The hall was open all the way down! When I told a teacher coming toward me what had happened, and that I had wondered if my mind was flipping out on me, he laughed. "The emergency door closed off the hallway. Your key would have fit it." Oh, how I hated locked doors! And here I was where every door I entered or left had to be locked. The only other time I saw that emergency door closed was a few years later when there was rumor of a riot.

Mr. O'Malley, the tall, thin Irish assistant principal, came by the library one morning and pushed his glasses up on his nose as he asked me to substitute in a County Boys' room while the teacher was away. I expected the County Boys to be more dangerous than the others. They had committed serious crimes and were waiting to be tried as

Teachah Don't Know Nothin'

adults. I was a little apprehensive as I walked to the classroom.

As I was sitting at the desk while the County Boys were all working quietly I realized the door was locked from the inside. I had the keys in my pocket, but had no idea which key fit the door. If a fight or some other kind of emergency occurred, I'd be in trouble.

I kept my hand on my pocket, feeling the keys. Slowly I began to relax. Before long I discovered that the County Boys were just like other kids in the school. In fact, they were more mature and well behaved, and as the day progressed we became friends. I thought they were easier to manage because they knew they were going to be in the detention center for a long time and had just settled in.

I had been reading a book about differences in cultural responses of Caucasians, Blacks, Mexicans, and Puerto Ricans. Later in the day I read aloud from it. The boys listened attentively to the anecdotes the author used as examples and in every case they knew how each culture would respond and a lot more about differences between the cultures than I did.

All the classrooms for the County Boys were self-contained, meaning the kids stayed in the same classroom all day, out only for lunch and gym. When I said, "OK, boys, its time for gym," I got an unexpected response.

"Boys! Don't call us boys! That's racist!"
"What are you then, if you're not boys?"
"We're inmates, criminals."
One of them said in a quiet voice, "We're men."

Chapter Sixteen

I ignored him and smiled as I said, "I'm not going to call you inmates or criminals. Let's go, guys." That worked.

Most teachers called the boys Gentlemen, but that wasn't a word I was used to using, and it sure didn't seem appropriate. As I became more relaxed with a group of boys, I called them Cutie, Handsome, Honey, Sweetheart, Little One (especially some of the big guys), or Big Guy (to a small kid), anything fun or endearing that came to mind at the time.

Before Mr. O'Malley told me the County Boys were too dangerous to bring to the library for tutoring, Norman told me his pimp story. He said he couldn't write, so I wrote for him to copy. Norman was a short, handsome, light-skinned black boy with shining eyes.

PIMPIN' AIN'T EASY, BUT NORMAN'S GOTTA DO IT

When I'm on the streets, I be dressed and draped (with jewelry). I got three main freaks, one named Keisha, one named Paige, and the other named Trisha. And this other little skeezer, she ain't really my freak, just a little git-along freak, get action and leave. They get mad when I don't come see them and when I do come see them they want to cuss and fuss and don't want to give up no action. Then I tell them that pimpin' ain't easy, but God sent me here to do it. I dress them, keep them in nice things, and some of them I like and some of them I love, but I ain't gonna mention no name cause it might go to their heads. One thing I like about them, when we pimp out of my 5-0 Mustang G.T., we be lookin' deft, me and my women.

Teachah Don't Know Nothin'

I like Keisha the most of all of them, so she's the one I'm gonna keep, my main lady. I'm gonna keep the other ones, just in case something go wrong with me and Keisha, keep them as back up.

So to be a pimp, you gotta look out for your women. So, like I said before, pimpin' ain't easy, but I gotta do it. Pimpin' Norm

Norman said his bond was two million dollars. He would be tried as an adult when he reached seventeen, so he wouldn't be pimping again any time soon.

Kenneth was a tall, skinny, good-looking County Boy. "I'll tell you the story about my snake skin hat, but you have to write it."

SNAKE SKIN HAT

My hat cost $96. It was a snakeskin hat, python skin. A Chicago Bulls hat with a python snake and cobra head right in front on each side of the Chicago Bulls. I had it made at the Candy Box across from CVS. (Chicago Vocational School).

I was at a game at CVS and I leaned back laughing and a boy grabbed my hat off my head. I was high and didn't see who grabbed it.

The next week I went up to CVS and this dude on the basketball team named West Side - I don't know his real name - had it on. I was about to do something I would regret. I was about to shoot him with the .38 in my pocket. I took it out and pointed it at him. But my friend Cubby stopped me. He said, "Let's go ask him for it." And lucky for him, he gave it back.

Chapter Seventeen

Unlike other schools, where you see kids walking casually in the hallways, students at Audy lined up against the walls, their hands in their pockets or behind their backs. They wore khaki-colored pants and white tee shirts with birds on the front, birds such as owls and cardinals that indicated the kid's section. Classrooms were on second floor, and the sections on third, fourth, and fifth.

Often when I walked through the halls and passed lines of boys, one or more of them would ask if they could come to the library and write for me. Sometimes they would sneak to me a drawing, or a story to be typed.

Many times the kids would sneak paper and pencils to section and write at night. Frank was one of them. He was sixteen, tall, mature, creative, with two children, a girlfriend, a mother and brothers and sisters that he felt were his responsibility. One morning I saw him in the hall

Teachah Don't Know Nothin'

as he was going to class. He said, "I got some papers for you."

When I went to get him later for our reading session his teacher said, "He can't go with you today. He hasn't done any work, just sits in here writing stuff for you. If he can't do my work, he can't write for you."

Frank had stood up when I entered the room. "Please, Mr. Cronin, let me go just this one time."

"Sit down, McGee." Mr. Cronin's tone was firm.

After I left the room I remembered Frank had said he had some papers for me. Oh, what if Mr. Cronin saw them and ripped them up like he did another kid's writing? I rushed back and asked if he had any of Frank's work for me. He didn't. I breathed a little easier, but wondered what happened to Frank's writing.

I made sure to be in the hallway when the kids were lined up to go to section at the end of the day, and when I saw Frank, he grinned and called to an attendant. The attendant turned to face the wall, unbuttoned his shirt, and pulled out pages of Frank's writings and drawings. So Frank was not only a favorite with me, he was with the attendants, too.

Frank was an excellent artist. He drew animals with different kinds of heads and bodies. His writing disturbed me. What a life he had, and no way to escape the Chicago Housing Authority project buildings. The following is a short sample of what Frank wrote.

> PLACE OF MISERY
> Dear Lord, I write unto you.
> Help me, Lord, to be free.

Chapter Seventeen

Free is a bird that flies above the sea.
Lord, Oh Lord, you shall help me,
Help me be free internally.
As we're between this brick wall,
Oh Lord, Oh Lord,
I want to break them all.
But, no Lord, no Lord,
Help me be free,
Free from this place of misery,
'Cause life indoors for several weeks
Is like living in hell internally.
But Lord, my Lord,
Help me to be free.
I pray unto thee
In the House of Misery.

The day before Frank was to be released he said, "Mrs. Oglesby, when I write to you, if I forget your name, can I call you Mother?"

I added Frank's writings to our books, which were growing in number. I usually took a number of the books with me when I was substituting in classrooms. In one class most of the students came in and got to work, but one guy looked like he didn't intend to do anything except cause trouble. I motioned for him to come to the desk and gave him one of the books to read. He began reading, and asked, "Is this by the County Boys?" Then he became involved in the reading, and laughed at something he read, and another guy went over. I gave him a book to read. Gradually, all the books were out.

Teachah Don't Know Nothin'

In a County Boys room I handed the noisiest kid a book and told him to read. Within minutes, all the books were out. One kid grabbed a book from another and almost started a fight. Someone started reading a rap, and a few others began saying it with him. One guy got a wastebasket for a drum, and hit the table with another hand, and they were reading the rap and getting rhythm to it. Then they started singing their own raps.

When I asked one guy if he would write his rap, another said he could write, too. Within a few minutes, the room was silent. Two boys who had worked together brought their rap to me and read it.

GANG VIOLENCE
Gang violence, we couldn't keep it silence,
To stop peer pressure, teen-agers join a gang.
Once you get in a gang, you're not the same
And on street corners is where you often hang.
The opposition come and shoot you up,
And the police are watching and they won't bust it up.
You say people don't care what you do,
You have just killed one or two opposition.
People of America should hate it, but they don't give a damn.
They put us behind the door and all we hear is slam.
Most of your role models are nothin' but thugs.
Gang bangers I know are smart and street-wise.
But when it come to education, some just close their eyes.
But there's a way we all can survive.

Chapter Seventeen

We don't have to be in a gang to stay live.
As you read this rhyme, made by me and Eddie "B",
 I hope you will see, that one day we all could be free.
W-O-R-D!!!!!!
 By Gary And Eddie B

I was so excited with the words they'd written about ending gang violence that I went straight to Mrs. Kapusic, showed her the rap, telling her how great I thought it would be for our school newspaper. She read it and said, "All this talks about is violence. I don't think it belongs in the paper." After we talked about it for a while she reluctantly decided to include it.

Some time after the boys had written the rap I was walking down the hall while the County Boys were lined up for class and a kid said, "Eddie B got a new name. Goodyear."

"Goodyear?" I asked.

"Yeah, you know, the blimp. Eddie B got so fat he look like a blimp now."

It was fun to watch the kids looking through a book to find their name or a familiar name on a page. Whatever the writing on that page, they thought it great and exciting. When I handed one boy his copy of his writing, he said, "Put it in the book, I want to go down in history."

I tried to accept anything the boys wrote, even when it was shocking to me. I didn't think they tried to shock, or wrote things that would be thought of as "bad" by adults. They didn't seem to think about adults or teachers reading their writing, but they made it clear that they didn't want judges and probation officers to read it.

Teachah Don't Know Nothin'

I believed they were writing because they had discovered fun in writing, and because their efforts were successful. Most of them had not had many successes in school. I didn't grade or criticize grammar or content. The fact that their work was "published" seemed to make the biggest impact. They liked to know other kids would read what they wrote.

Jimmy, a Yugoslavian gypsy, had learned to spell his name, but didn't know how to write most numerals, how to write his birth date, and didn't know the alphabet. He hadn't gone to school at all until he was about eleven, and very seldom went to school after that. If you're eleven and put in a class with twenty-five to thirty-five other kids, what's a teacher to do with you?

I helped him write a story, typed it, and helped him read it. Once, when he came in I said, "Oh, Jimmy, I don't know whether I can find your writing or not. Now, what will we do?"

He said, "That's OK." He reached down in his sock and pulled out his copy. By the end of that class he knew how to read every word.

The same thing happened the next day. I said, "Oh, Jimmy, I don't have it today for sure." He reached down and pulled it out. That happened three days in a row. Every day he had his writing with him. And every day he could read it a little better.

The one thing that had to be removed from our books was a poem written by a white kid about the Ku Klux Klan. I didn't want to put it in the books, but so far I'd included everything the boys wrote, so I added it.

Chapter Seventeen

Niggers will die,
Spicks will pay,
But out of the dark
Rises the KKK.
Save our land,
Join the Klan.

In every book where I put that poem, the kids would either mark all over it so it couldn't be read, or rip it from the book. I don't remember any comments about it.

Fingers said his nickname meant no hands because he had been shot in his hands and for a while couldn't use them. He was a good artist and I thought of his name as meaning he used his fingers well. Les held out a paper to Fingers and asked, "Will you draw me something?"

Fingers looked up, "You a Flake (opposing gang). I ain't drawing nothin' for you."

"I just want you to draw me a world, man." Les looked disappointed.

Fingers hesitated, then said, "Hold on. I gotta finish this and I'll do it." Wow! A gang member was helping a kid from another gang? That was hard to believe.

Some of the kids who were good at art liked to make covers for the books and illustrate the stories and poems. Little skinny Barry worked for days on making a cover for our book about babies. When he finished it to his satisfaction, he said, "Now, me and Ronald gonna write a book together."

Ronald said, "No, I'm gonna write it."

"No, I'm gonna write it." They argued about it awhile, then Barry said, "He gonna do one page and I'm gonna do

Teachah Don't Know Nothin'

another. Take them staples out, how we gonna write like this? It's our book. You gotta make two copies. How long it gonna take you to type it?"

I often wished I had help in putting the books together, and for one week, I had Marcus's help. He was above average in achievement, from Evanston. While I was substituting in his class he asked if he could help me in the library with the books. The day before he left, I saw him in line in the hallway. He motioned for me to come to him and sneaked an envelope to me. This is part of his letter.

Dear Mrs. Dee Oglesby,

I know we met in the wrong place, but then anyhow it probably was the best place. What I mean is I can work with you better in here than outside. I like you because you're a very lovely and kind woman. We can work together. From what I saw us do, plus you're easy to get along with. I never really met anybody such as you who can really understand my point of view about things. I know for a fact if we were together more often both of us could get things done. Example the school paper, the booklets that mean so much to you, etc. To tell the truth I really feel so special around you. I would love to work with you on my free time on the outside, if its O.K. with you. We could work at a library if you wanted to because I want to help you finish what we started. I don't want anybody else to help you but me.

Your Devoted Friend, Marcus D. Brown

Marcus was released the next day and I never saw him again.

Chapter Seventeen

Not only were the students at Audy excited about writing their stories, people outside the school showed excitement when I talked about the writing the boys did. My friend Eileen wanted to interview me for National Public Radio. I was somewhat apprehensive but did the interview anyhow, hoping Mr. Hahn wouldn't hear it. He did, on the way to school on teachers' in-service day. He decided I would speak to the teachers for the afternoon session. After my talk about what I was doing with the reading and writing - or writing and reading - he divided the teachers into groups to discuss how they could implement my methods in their classrooms. I should have anticipated the response. These teachers were "old pros." Most of them had taught there many years, and here was a new teacher gaining recognition, and Mr. Hahn saying they should do in their classrooms what she was doing.

Almost all comments were negative. The teachers said the writings were not teacher-directed, did not stress morality, and did not help the kids see the harmful effect of crime on their lives. They also said the writings were racist.

I left that day feeling discouraged, yet I still believed that writing about their own experiences helped the kids think about their lives, and certainly helped them learn to read since what they were reading had relevance for them.

The next day I was substituting in a class of the top students in the school and had some of the books with me. The boys began reading and discussing the stories, and I mentioned that most of the teachers thought the books were harmful. The following is a compilation of what those boys wrote about the books.

Teachah Don't Know Nothin'

I think you should be able to write whatever you want because also the 1st Amendment says freedom of the press and they could write whatever they want so why couldn't we!

The books about boys in this center are okay because they help the new kids like me know how they feel and it helps ease me down. It makes me feel like one of them because at least I know I will get a chance to start life over. Also it shows that I am not the only one that's scared. My two weeks here were the worst days of my life and you hear the stories of these kids staying in here for months and they say it is nothing. So when you think about these kids, you feel sorry for them instead of yourself so your days pass quicker. The kids' writings make you think at least I'll get out of here and back home. So now I just want to get out of here.

These books are an expression of a part of society that people don't want to hear or see. For the first time people who have never been able to express themselves, can say what they feel, not what they were told to feel. Things that people fear they don't want to face.

What the students wrote echoed my own opinions, but even as I dealt with disappointment at the teachers' reactions, I was getting some good responses outside school. One came from my daughter, Marianne, who had heard on television about an international teacher's award being offered by the Kohl Educational Foundation. She followed through with the process of nominating me. To

Chapter Seventeen

receive that award was one of the greatest events of my life. It seemed to validate for me that I wasn't just playing games and having fun, but that others thought what I was doing with children was valuable. I was especially please when Mr. Hahn came for the presentation. He seldom made any comments about my work, but at his retirement dinner he said to me, "Keep doing what you're doing. It's important."

Soon after the teachers' meeting, the assistant principal informed me that a classroom was being readied for me. No longer would I be tutoring students, I'd be teaching grammar to rotating high school classes. The school population was increasing so rapidly that more classroom teachers were required. He told me to check with other teachers and see if I could find some grammar textbooks. As he left he said, "This is the end of your program." I thought to myself, do you want to bet?

Once again, I had nothing to work with except what I could find myself. The classroom had been used as a storage room, had no windows or ventilation, and no closets or closed storage space except for a small metal coat cabinet, two file cabinets, and long metal shelves. I bought three locks for the coat cabinet before the boys told me what kind of lock to get that they couldn't open. One wall was covered with a large blackboard and another with a bulletin board. Even plants wouldn't grow there, since there was so much darkness and no sunlight.

I made a booklet with suggestions for writing an autobiography, which included a list of recommended topics. On the first day of class each student received a

Teachah Don't Know Nothin'

booklet for writing and an instruction booklet. Little explanation was needed before the boys got to work writing and decorating covers for their books.

Now I had ten students at a time instead of two, so I knew my days of typing all the stories were over, but when the boys began writing poetry, I typed it, mounted it on colored construction paper and placed it on the bulletin board. In a short time the bulletin board was covered with poetry, some of it illustrated.

The students enjoyed writing their own books, and if a student knew his release date in time to tell me, I took his class work to the release clerk so he could take it home with him.

Mark was a tall, good-looking white boy. He came to the desk and said softly, "If I write my story, can you hide it for me?"

"I can put it in the desk drawer and lock it each night."

He whispered to me that his story was about a man who put him into prostitution. Each day he came for his book, pushed his desk away from the others, and wrote his story.

Leroy strutted into class his first day, looked me square in the eye, pushed his shoulders back, and said, "I'm a hustler."

I said right back to him, "What's a hustler?"

"Don't do no school work. Don't do no kind of work. I don't never do no work for no white man. Just make money."

"Do you mean you don't ever expect to have a job or work for anybody?"

Chapter Seventeen

"That's right. And I don't go to school. I got street knowledge."

"How will you get money to live?"

"Any way I can. Sell drugs, pimp, steal, anything. I got people working for me. And we don't learn no school learnin', just got street knowledge."

"Well, that makes a problem for us," I said. "You'll be bored sitting here doing nothing, and if you begin talking with the other guys, you'll be making problems for them. So, we'll have to find something for you to do that's interesting. Can you think of anything?"

"Nope."

"It's not really learning, so maybe you could staple these papers together for me."

"OK."

Collating and making booklets kept him busy for a few days. Then I asked him, "Can you read?"

"Yep."

"I have a rap I'd like to have recorded. If you take the tape recorder over to the corner of the room it won't bother the others if you read it aloud into the tape recorder."

I gave him Eddie B's rap on gang violence. He looked it over, and came to the desk. "What is this? This kid says you gonna get rid of gang violence. I told you I'm a hustler. I can't read nothin' like this."

That plan didn't work, so I gave him some paper, lettering stencils, and markers. "Here, see what you can do with this."

He worked with them for a little while before he began looking bored. I said, "Take the tape recorder and go to the

199

Teachah Don't Know Nothin'

back of the room. Get two desks together and interview the guys, one at a time. Ask any questions you want to ask."

He liked that idea. He began, "This is station WGCI. What is yo name? What is you in here for?" He did that for a few days, then came in, picked up his booklet and began writing.

Tim was a shy child who loved art. He came to the desk one day with a picture he had drawn of a sexy girl in a swimsuit so skimpy it was almost as though she had nothing on. He asked, "Can I put it on the bulletin board?"

I looked at the drawing and knew it was not suitable. I said, "If you take this black marker and outline your drawing it will show up more."

A few minutes later he returned. "Now, can I put it on the bulletin board?"

I was trying to delay him until the end of the period. "I think you might want to add color to your picture. That would make it look prettier."

As the class was leaving he returned with his colored picture and I let him put it up. As soon as he left, before the next class came in, I took it down. When he asked about it the next day, I told him he had made the kind of picture all the boys liked to take upstairs, that if he wanted to make more of that kind of picture, I'd keep them and put them in my own book. He made two more and didn't ask again that they be placed on the bulletin board.

One day Joey delivered a note to me at the desk that said, "I like you, do you like me? Am I quiet in your class?" No name was signed to the note. After I read it I put it in my desk drawer. Next day, he gave me another note. This time

Chapter Seventeen

I watched and saw Joey whispering with Chester, so I knew who had sent the notes. The next note said, "Can I have a date with you? Will you give me your telephone number? Can I take you out to eat? I like you." No name. I folded the paper and put it in the drawer.

Next day, Joey was first to come in the room. He said, "Chester's got a crush on you."

I smiled and said, "Oh, he has good taste."

"What?" His questioning eyes let me know he didn't know what I meant.

I said, "He chose somebody pretty nice to have a crush on."

"Oh," he said as he walked away. Later I noticed the boys giggling and whispering to each other. When they saw me looking at them, Joey pointed to Chester and said, "He's got a crush on you."

I walked back to them. "Didn't any of you guys have a crush on an older woman yet? Most guys sometime while they're young get crushes on older women. I think Chester chose a pretty fine older woman to have a crush on, don't you?" The snickering stopped.

After that Chester brought up his own notes. I was old enough to be his grandmother, and he didn't know how to let me know he liked me except to write notes as if I were a girlfriend. He was soon released, and I never heard from him again.

Otis was at Audy for a long time. He faced major charges, murder being one of them, so he would likely be tried as an adult. He was a short, stocky black boy who said he didn't want to be in school, he didn't want to be in my room. Then he would cause major disturbances among the boys. He did some things to help me, like staple papers together, but when I mentioned work he said he didn't do work in school, that he didn't need it. The day before he was going to court he came to the desk and said, "I need a good report for the judge. If you give me a good report the judge will let me go. My cousin got killed and I want to go to the funeral."

I said, "Oh, Otis, I thought you knew. Teachers don't give grades and reports. They just report on what you do. Students earn their reports. If you want good grades and good reports on your behavior, you must think ahead so you can earn them."

The report I gave to the judge told of the disturbances Otis routinely caused. He was not released. I would have been happy to have him out of the class, but he stayed at least another thirty days before going to court again. One day I told him I thought he had good leadership qualities that could help him to do a lot of good for the world and for his people.

"What'd you mean, in the gangs?"

"Well, I wasn't thinking about gangs," I said. "I was thinking about life in general."

The other kids interrupted and the conversation with Otis ended. Within a few minutes, he reached over the desk and got some writing paper, some typing paper, and a pink sheet like the ones I used to make the writing booklets. He folded them in half, then picked up a new folder and asked me to cut it for him. "I want to make a book."

Chapter Seventeen

I told him to hold on, maybe I could find something better for a cover than the folder. I found a piece of orange board about the consistency of the folder. He grinned. As he folded the board over, the papers stuck out a little from the cover. When I suggested we trim the paper, he said, "No, I don't want it trimmed. How do you get these papers stapled in here?"

I found the saddle stapler for him and he stapled the papers upside down and a little off center. I said, "Here, let's turn it over and you won't have a problem." I gave him the staple remover and he put the pages together perfectly. He looked over with a big smile on his face, and tried to push a guy away from a chair at my desk. There were already three guys working close to the desk, so I pulled a chair up to the file cabinet beside the desk and said, "Here, we'll find a place for these books and you can sit here."

He sat down and asked for the lettering stencils. The big stencil was too big and the little one too little. He wanted to write "Knowledge" on the cover. While all this was taking place one of the guys said he could make bubble letters. He had written his name on the desk in pencil with beautiful bubble letters. I said, "If you guys can make such beautiful lettering, why do you want these plain stencils?"

Otis said, "I'll write it myself. How do you spell knowledge?" I wrote knowledge on a piece of paper and gave it to him. He printed the letters on his cover.

I said, "Let me show you something," and took a marker and made little straight lines close together to "color" around the letters. "That will make it shine, but it takes a lot of time."

Teachah Don't Know Nothin'

Otis said, "I know how to do that and it won't take much time." He drew his lines, and said, "I ruined it! I spelled it wrong." He was trying to write "school" and had left the *c* out and had only *sh* there, a little uneven.

"That's no problem," I said. "Put the *c* up here and the other letters sort of scrambled."

One of the boys said, "What's the matter, Otis, don't you know how to spell school?"

Otis said angrily, "Listen to him! I just told you I left out the *c* and he said I don't know how to spell school." While he finished writing the title, he kept muttering about the kid saying he didn't know how to spell. Then he held his book up to a kid sitting beside him and said, "What does that say?"

I held my breath until the kid said, "School Knowledge." Otis put the colored lines around the word school and finished just as the period was over. He was so pleased with his book that I couldn't suggest he leave it in his folder until Monday. The attendant let him take it upstairs. Monday he brought it back full of stories.

Another black boy, Daniel - a small quiet boy - came to me almost in tears. He pointed to one of the other boys and whined, "He just called me a name." He wouldn't say what the other boy had called him.

"Does the word start with an *N*?" I asked.

"Yes, and the dictionary says it's the lowest form of a person."

"Oh, I don't think you'll find that definition in the dictionary."

Chapter Seventeen

Webster's dictionary, of course, does not say that, though it does say the term is derogatory. A few days later he was looking over my "street talk" dictionary and found the word. My list did say that one meaning of nigger is "the lowest kind of a person," but there were other meanings too. For Daniel, the damage had been done. His opinion of himself had been confirmed.

White juvenile offenders felt that they were superior to the blacks in the detention center, and did not hesitate to make it known that they thought they were superior. They usually managed to intimidate the blacks. That way, even though they were in the minority, they were safe. Often they indicated that they were Satan Worshipers, with psychic powers. Then the susceptible black kids, who tended to be superstitious, were afraid of them.

Occasionally friendships formed on a surface level between white and black boys, but I thought there would be no follow-through with those friendships after they left Audy. Blacks, in general, did not like the white kids and did not trust them.

When one of my classes contained no white boys, I told the guys I was writing a paper and needed to know what black boys really think of white boys. They talked freely once they felt there would be no repercussions from their comments. Below are a few of their remarks.

"White kids are weird, I hate them motherfuckers. They rule the god-dammed world."

"They get your ass locked up."

"They call us nigger. They act goofy. They don't want us around them. They think they better than us."

Teachah Don't Know Nothin'

"They ain't into music, not deep into music."

"They don't know how to dress. They wear cheap gym shoes, not Jordans, Air Force 11, and all that stuff. They don't wear hats like we do. We dress jazzy. They dress casual, and we dress rap."

"They're nasty, real nasty." (I pushed for what they meant by nasty.) "They have oral sex. That's disgusting. It's nasty."

"The Puerto Ricans are pretty much like us. They OK."

"Ain't no white gonna be a real friend."

Chapter Eighteen

Through a chain of circumstances that included a planned computer room we thought we were going to get and didn't, I moved from the windowless room. The new room had a whole row of big windows, a toilet for the boys, and a very large teacher prep room, and walls freshly painted bright yellow. An absolutely beautiful classroom! I felt like a bird released from its cage.

A bright new room and a new assignment: a self-contained class. The prospect excited me. I wanted to try out my theories about what would make a great self-contained room, where the students could stay in the same room all day and stick with a project long enough to finish it.

Over the years, I'd envisioned what I would like for a self-contained classroom for older kids. Since my last such room, I'd formed new ideas about what would make a better environment for learning. I would soon retire, so I expected this to be my final chance to prove to myself that my ideas could work. I'd already collected many of the items I wanted to use.

I made a cubbyhole surrounded by book shelves with a variety of books I thought would be interesting to the boys - books on science, astrology, world religions, art, and so forth, and a table and chairs in the center to complete the reading section. Four desks pulled together made a table for the plastic-wading-pool-filled-with-dirt garden. I copied sections from textbooks of low levels of math, science, and social studies work. I found a big supply of cardstock and made "blue books" for writing, and assembled a quantity of the instruction booklets for writing autobiographies. A long table at the back of the room held art supplies, an electronic keyboard, adding machine, calculator, and a guitar. A TV with a tape player was ready for watching specialty and instructional films. On a nearby desk were a few old typewriters and an outdated computer. I stockpiled some games and puzzles, and arranged the desks in a semi-circle with my desk completing the circle.

The night before the first day of class, I rehearsed a speech on the tape recorder I always kept handy. My students were to be high school boys of different ages and levels of ability. My requirements were simple. The boys would have in their folders the blue book for writing and a few other academic assignments that would take little time to complete. Since grades were required, to receive an A, each day they must write at least a page, complete the few

Chapter Eighteen

assignments, keep busy, be respectful to everyone, and be quiet when I was talking to the class.

My speech spoke of their freedom to make choices, even while locked up. They had the freedom to follow the rules, or break the rules, and they had the freedom to choose their reactions to situations. I even said that if they knew they were going to die, they had the freedom to choose how they would act and feel at that time. And on the streets they could choose whether to join a gang or whether they would do what the leaders of the gang told them to do. They would reap the consequences of their choices, but they could make choices wherever they were. Maybe I felt it important to talk about freedom because the boys so often felt they had no choices at Audy - no choices about what to eat, when to get up, when to go to bed, or when to take baths. Their lives were regimented and they resented it.

When I gave the talk, the boys were quiet and seemed to listen attentively. The morning passed smoothly. Afternoon was a different story - total chaos, or as the kids would say, OC, out of control. They argued over the equipment, and made an inordinate amount of noise. What had gone wrong?

As the students left that afternoon, I sat at my desk with my head in my hands. Why wasn't my plan working as I thought it would?

Evidently I'd given too many alternatives at once to kids who were used to following directions instead of choosing for themselves. I removed most of the articles that made noise - keyboard, guitar, television and other equipment and stored them in the prep room.

Teachah Don't Know Nothin'

The next morning as each student came in, I handed him his folder and pointed to a desk. After they were all seated and quiet, I apologized for not being more aware of what was happening the day before and explained that I thought I'd given them too much freedom too soon. Then we talked. How could everyone have a chance to use the equipment, and still accomplish our academic work? One kid said he thought work in the folders should be done first thing in the morning with no talking.

Shawn - a tall, husky, light-skinned boy from Cabrini Green, a housing project with the worst of reputations - fired back, "What you want from me? Finish high school, go to college, get married, have kids, a white house with a picket fence in the suburbs?"

His was the only outburst. Most of the suggestions the boys made sounded so mature I was surprised as much as I was pleased. They suggested that the guitar be played in the bathroom, that sound on the keyboard could be turned low, and that we discuss which video to play.

Within a month or two my self-contained class worked in such an orderly way I could sit at my desk for long periods of time, and be available, but not have to give any instructions.

The kids made signs for the door: THE SPOT (the name for the place where they held their gang meetings); DO NOT DISTURB, THIS CLASS HARD AT WORK; and FOR THE LOVE OF THIS CLASS.

We planted our garden and watched things grow, sometimes watching with a magnifying glass. We watched the new detention center building go up and figured time

Chapter Eighteen

and costs. We counted the hundreds of little plants being set on the hill nearest our window, discussed how long before they would cover all the ground, why the specific plant was chosen, how much each plant would cost, preparation of the soil, and pay for the workers. We noted the races of the workers: black, white, and Latino.

When a child showed a special interest, I made it my business to find the materials he needed. For instance, one wanted to design his future home, and I was able to find books, drafting paper, and tools for him.

Some of the boys could sit intently for hours with a puzzle. Others didn't have the patience to work even a simple one. Sometimes they would work together on a puzzle. Then we glued them to cardboard and hung them on the wall, with the names of the ones who worked them. I could learn a lot about a child by watching how he worked a puzzle.

The boys wrote and presented plays, also music and poetry programs - first for our class, and then for other classes.

One of the plays was about a couple of undercover cops on assignment to break into a drug ring, but the main players were the drug dealers: the "Big Man," the "right hand man" called Dollar Bill, and "Too Short," the guy on the street selling dime bags. While we were practicing reading the play, Shawn looked over at David and said, "What is this? You can't read nothin'. How come you can read this so good?"

Another play opened with a street fight where a black boy gets shot by a white guy. The other scenes show the

Teachah Don't Know Nothin'

victim's best friends and girlfriend and mother dealing with their grief. The two friends have this conversation:

Rickey: Damn, man, we let him kill him. We let him kill him! We won't see him any more! No more! No more good times anymore! No more great laughs. No more walking together. No more looking for girls. No double dates. No more roller-skating together. The fun we had together, it's all dead! And Darric's dead!

Ronny: (Hugging Rickey) At least we know he's with God, safe from evil and sorrow.

In scene eight, at the wake, the preacher says,

My people, as the scripture of Genesis says, everyone must go. And we are all going to go to dust sometime. But after we die, the question is, where are we going? Darric was a treasure to our lives and the people around him. Now, we know that he had some problems at some time, and when he saw Jesus, he was saved and changed for the better.

After the wake, Ronny takes the girlfriend home. This scene takes place in the car:

Cathy: How should I live now, Ronny?

Ronny: We must live the best we can, the way we've been doing.

Cathy: And how is that?

Ronny: For each other.

Cathy: I never told you, but I love you, Ronny.

Ronny: I love you, too, Cathy, but you're Darric's woman and I can't stab my best friend in the back, even if he is dead.

Chapter Eighteen

Cathy: I would think that what Darric would want out of us is for you to protect me while he's away.

Ronny: Do you think you can handle me or me handle you?

Cathy: I think we can handle each other together and love each other. (She kisses him.)

Ronny: (In a daze, kissing back) Well, it's of consequence that we can see each other.

The boys titled this play "Strange People the Next Color." In the final scene the two friends track down the white boy who killed their friend, and have the gun pulled to shoot him, but they stop to debate whether to pull the trigger or not. One wants the honky to bite the dust. The other argues for letting him suffer a prison sentence before he goes to hell, and they end up calling the police - a happy ending.

It did not surprise me that the boys had the best friend pair up with the deceased's girlfriend. The subject of girls ranked right up there with gangs - main topics of conversation.

Sometimes the girlfriends would come and stand on Ogden Avenue, outside the window, so the boys could see them. The boys, when I let them, made big signs to hold in the window.

If a guy spotted girls outside, he'd say "Broads!" The others would rush to the window to see if their girlfriends were there.

Through the years I experimented with a number of methods of keeping order. In this classroom I made a large sign for the wall. "NO FIGHTS. NO REAL FIGHTS. NO

Teachah Don't Know Nothin'

PLAY FIGHTS. NO WORD FIGHTS." If I thought the guys were getting close to a fight I'd point to the sign, and sometimes that would stop the disturbance. Sometimes the students would point to the sign if they thought a fight was beginning.

Soon after I posted the sign Eddie came in and stared at the board a few minutes, then pointed his stubby finger at it and said, "What's a word fight?" He jerked his head around and said, "Oh, you mean a argument. You ought to write no arguments up there."

"OK," I said, "you can write it."

With a serious look on his face, he said, "Why I'm gonna write that up there? I argue all the time."

I also found the "anh" sound effective, as I had at Bartelme, for stopping an impending fight or keeping a student from doing something I didn't want him to do, usually something simple like starting to go to the window.

One day the boys came from gym and were loud and disorderly. I decided not to say anything and see what would happen. Chico, a short, energetic and talkative boy, came to the desk and asked for something and I kept on with my writing and didn't look at him. He said, "Are you ignoring me?" I nodded yes. He said OK and sat down. The class was soon quiet and busy.

Another day the class was noisy and I wrote on a big sheet of paper in big letters, "SILENCE." I walked around to each kid and showed the sign. It worked.

Occasionally, I'd notice a fight starting and say, "We don't do that in here." Nearly always, just those words stopped the trouble. The counselor, Mr. Ray, had said many

Chapter Eighteen

times about fights, "One's scared, and one don't want to fight." Usually, all it took to stop a fight was to catch it early and give both boys a way out so they didn't lose face.

I usually got at least one new student each week. On his first day in my class, a big husky guy named Anton stood with his elbows propped on the windowsill, looking out at the world. He refused to sit down. "You can't make me do nothin'. I'm bigga than you."

I'd learned many years before about "bigga."

"So-o-o?" I said with a grin. "Bigga don't count in fights."

He laughed and sat down.

The next day he came in with a deck of cards, pulled four chairs around a desk, got three other boys, and began shuffling cards. I said, "We don't do that in here." I waited while he put the cards in his pocket. In a few minutes they were back in business. I walked over to him again and said, "I told you, we don't do that in here." Again I waited while he put the cards in his pocket.

The third time I said, "Now you have a choice. You can put those cards in your pocket and leave them there, and you can take them with you. Or you can give them to me to keep for you until class is over. If you start playing again, those cards are mine."

He looked at me with a grin of admiration. "I bet you still trimmin', too."

"That's a new word for me. What does it mean?"

He blushed.

"Oh, you mean you think I'm still having sex! Thanks, that's a new word for our dictionary."

215

Teachah Don't Know Nothin'

I walked back to my desk. Tyrone followed me. With a big grin on his dark face, he said, "Mrs. Oglesby, I really do respect you. You sure stand on your potentiality."

Frequently the new boys discussed whether I was afraid or not. They'd say "She afraid," or "She ain't afraid." I especially liked hearing, "She ain't afraid of nobody."

Students did occasionally attack a teacher. When my classes were still held in the windowless room and I had the door open for ventilation one afternoon, a boy ran in, slammed the door, and began knocking over desks and throwing things around the room. My class was working, and I was supposed to have had the door closed. The door locked when the boy slammed it shut. Immediately Mrs. Sullivan was knocking on it. "Let me in! Let me at him! He threw a chair at me."

I looked at the kid who was now standing in the corner against the wall and realized he was frightened. I called to Mrs. Sullivan, "As soon as he cleans up the mess he made in here, I'll open the door."

By the time he'd cleaned up, Mrs. Sullivan was back in her classroom. All classrooms had telephones, so I called and told her I'd had an attendant take him upstairs.

Once when I was away the kids caused a substitute teacher to walk out of class in the middle of the day. The attendants told me that as he left he said, "I quit. There's not one kid there worth trying to help. They're punishing me by putting me in here."

The attendants asked, "Who - who is punishing you?"

"God," he said. "And those kids shouldn't be in school! They should be locked up! They're criminals."

Chapter Eighteen

Shawn, who was in the Audy because he had shot at a policeman and was in my class a long time, later told me what really happened. The substitute told them he belonged to the El Rukins gang. Once a member of a gang, always a member, and there were no El Rukins in the class at the time, only members of opposition gangs. I'd like to have been a fly on the wall to see the students' reactions to the substitute's comment.

Over and over the kids made comments about which gang I belonged to, or hinted that I might want to join their gang. I usually grinned and said nothing.

I discovered a storage closet with leftover stuff from other schools - book cases, file cabinets, books, adding machines, special papers and other great finds. I got the boys to help me move some things to the classroom, and let them paint a big metal cabinet bright yellow. Shawn asked if he could paint a picture on the side. He did a great job of painting the Chicago skyline. Underneath, in big letters, he wrote "Mrs. Ogleby World." I hugged him and told him what a great job he had done. Chicago, the best and the worst, was indeed my world, though I hadn't thought of it that way until I saw Shawn's painting.

Shawn also drew a portrait of me. Over the picture he wrote my name; under it he wrote, "Mrs. Want To Know It All."

When the students went off to gym, I often pulled the chairs that were scattered all over the room into a circle and included my chair to complete the circle. The kids would return, take a seat, and sit quietly and respectfully. Then I'd say something like, "Listen to this," and I'd read a poem or

Teachah Don't Know Nothin'

story one of them had written, or read an excerpt or article I thought they'd find interesting. Sometimes we'd discuss some problem that had come up within the class or between students. Sometimes I'd tell them about my adventures in the Canadian wilderness, or about my experience in a plane crash in the mountains of Kentucky.

Once I told the story of the plane crash and how the man whose car we flagged down seemed afraid to give us a ride. Maurice looked almost scared when he asked, "If you'd a been black, would he a picked you up?"

I thought about my relatives in the mountains of North Carolina who belonged to the Ku Klux Klan, and felt afraid too. I answered, "I surely hope so."

One day I mentioned to Mr. Franklin, director of the lock-up sections, the impact the circle had on the students. He said in the gangs it's called the "Circle of Equal Status." I did know the boys had spoken of 360-degree circles - that's how the gang members sat when they had discussions. I never figured out whether it was the gang association that caused the boys to behave so well when we sat in a circle. Sometimes a student would refuse to sit in the circle, so we let him sit close, and usually before long he pulled his chair into the circle.

Many times my southern drawl caught the kids' attention. They'd ask something like, "Are you country?" I'd usually smile and say, "I'm a hillbilly." I wasn't really, but I had kin people who were, and I didn't want to just answer that I was from the south.

Shawn and a few of the boys were looking out the window one day when I heard him say, "Just look at him,

Chapter Eighteen

he don't even know how to walk. White people walk like they got a stick up they ass."

After a few minutes of listening to them make fun of the way white people do things, I said, "Shawn, what is this you guys are doing, making fun of white people in front of me?"

"Oh, Mrs. Oglesby, we ain't talkin' about you. You ain't white, you a hillbilly."

Another of the boys said, "No, she a nigger." That was an instance of the usually derogatory term used in a complimentary way.

Shawn said, "Mrs. Oglesby is like playing football, fun, tough, and have to work hard." A little later I was explaining something to one of the boys who didn't seem to understand my explanation. Shawn came over and said, "She don't talk like we talk. Let me explain it so you know what she mean."

Then he said, "Mrs. Oglesby, it's good you ain't prejudiced. I'd a probably did something to you by now. I got a secret way of finding out who prejudice and who not. That's how I found out Mr. O'Malley's prejudiced."

"A secret way?"

"Yeah, I just look um in the eyes."

I was pleased that Shawn thought I wasn't prejudiced. So often I'd wondered how much prejudice I had left in me. Over and over I'd been thankful that I was not born with black skin and all the problems that come with it in our society.

Chapter Nineteen

Brad, the art teacher gave me a stack of long strips of pink tag board, about 3 x 36 inches. When I gave them to the boys to see what they would do with them, they began writing their gang names and decorating them with gang symbols. At first I didn't know what was happening because I was ignorant about most of the gang stuff. They covered the wall over the bulletin board, and made a big sign that said, "WALL OF FAME." That's what they called the graffiti walls in their neighborhoods where they wrote all their names. When a guy tried to move another name to put his over it so his name and his gang would be highest, I told him no name was ever moved.

All gangs were represented, all mixed up, believe it or not. If there was even a slight sign of trouble, I let the boys know quickly that trouble meant everything would have to come down. I told them that my classroom was the only place in the building, from the basement through the ceiling, where they wouldn't get in trouble for talking or writing about gangs, and the reason was that I was studying about gangs at the university and needed to know as much as I could. My friend Flora had arranged for a grant and I was studying linguistics and culture.

I wondered if ever before rival gangs had been represented peacefully, all mixed up together on one wall. Frequently some kid would stick his head in the door to see if his name was still on the wall, or to see the name of somebody who had been released.

When one of the older attendants came in one afternoon and saw the wall, he told me it was gang stuff and he didn't like it. I was afraid he might make a report about it, so the next day I told the kids we'd have to remove the pink boards and only put up names without any gang signs.

Lavelle had his desk pulled up to mine making his name for the wall. I said, "Remember, no gang signs." He wrote his nickname, which at that time I didn't know was his gang name, then added "G.D." (Gangster Disciples). I shook my head.

He said, "How about if I add a 'N' (Nation)? Again I grinned and shook my head. He drew a heart with wings, and erased it when I shook my head. He drew a cross with "Love Mom," and I shook my head.

"Well, can I write numbers, '7' and '4'?" I knew the numbers represented the Gangster Disciples and again shook my head. He grinned, "Well, I tried to pull your leg

Chapter Nineteen

but it ain't movin'. I tried to geek you, but you know what time it is."

The students gave me copies of the gang knowledge they were required to learn. I put them in my locked desk drawer before taking them home. Jerome asked if I had a copy of the 'I Pledge.' I thought I'd found it, but he said, "This is the 'We Pledge.' I need the 'I Pledge.'" I didn't have the "I Pledge" so another student recited it while I wrote it for him.

Curtis and three other boys came to the desk with some writing they'd been working on. Curtis whispered, "Will you type this for us?" It was the Disciples' creed. They spoke in whispers as they told me how they wanted it typed. When anyone came close they stopped talking and hid their papers. They had four pages of secret gang information. I typed it, leaving blanks so they could draw the gang symbols.

I would never have believed there was so much to learn to belong to a gang. A dumb kid would never have made it. To be accepted at the beginning, a kid needed to learn certain knowledge. To move from one level to the next, he needed to learn more knowledge.

I had two gang books that I kept in the drawer, one for each of the major Chicago gangs. They included symbols, language, and literature (knowledge). Each sub-set or regional group within the two gangs individualized the material slightly, so there were many variations.

I soon became an "expert" on gangs. I attended a National Law Enforcement Gang Institute in California and another in Indianapolis. I gained a lot of general

Teachah Don't Know Nothin'

information, but found that the material in my collection was more comprehensive than that of the law enforcement people I met there. I did add a little to my collection. People get excited about adding to collections of all sorts - coins, stamps, or salt and peppershakers - and I got just as excited about adding to my collection of gang information.

Details about gang culture fascinated me. I felt driven to learn more - the same kind of intense desire to learn as when I first began to teach in the Chicago schools and wanted to learn the rhymes, language, and details about life in the ghettos.

Besides my mysterious craving to learn, I thought any knowledge I gained would help me understand more about what was happening with the kids - so I could work with them better.

I made sure the boys knew that if anything from the classroom caused any problem of any kind upstairs, on sections, their freedom to work on gang stuff in my classroom would quickly come to an end.

Frequently I did wonder if I should allow the work in class, but the boys were so serious about learning their gang knowledge that they worked hard to learn to write and read it - and these were students who seldom did any school reading or writing if they could avoid it.

Demond asked the same question many others asked. He was a fifteen-year-old, nice-looking, tall, brown-skinned boy. He said, "Mrs. Oglesby, how come you gettin' all this gang stuff?"

"I think it's important for somebody to collect gang information," I answered. "Someday there might not be any

Chapter Nineteen

gangs, and unless somebody makes a collection - a record - all this part of our culture will be lost."

"Always gonna be gangs," Demond said. "Our Nation don't die, we multiply."

"Well, maybe gangs will change. Anyhow, it seems important to me to collect as much as I can and learn as much as I can."

The next day Demond came to class with an introduction he'd written for our book of gang art:

> This book was designed to express today's gang culture in hope that one day there will not be any gangs. I don't believe there is a single boy out there who has not wanted to join a club where there wasn't any adults to tell them what to do. Yes, those were the days when a child would do anything to join so that others would respect him as well as to gain popularity. Clubs and gangs are the same things, well technically, yes they are! Clubs are what sparks that flame that nudges you on what way to decide in joining a gang. If the club you belong to when you were a youth was a good club like the Boys Club, then most likely you'd say "No, I don't want to join." Seven out of ten percent will say this. Now if the club you belong to as a youth ran wild and wasn't really serving no purpose but to gain respect and almost always getting in trouble, then nine out of ten percent will say "Yes, I'll join." The next page is a short story also written for the purpose of expressing this imaginative book. Enjoy!

Teachah Don't Know Nothin'

IN THE BEGINNING
A long time ago when there was no gangs there was a boy named Jeff who lived in a small town on a street named Dirt Road. Jeff was the president of a club called The Lords. Now down on Branch Drive there was another club called the Gangsters. This club was a peaceful club until one day they had to walk through the Gangsters' territory. Now the Gangsters were strict on certain rules and they wanted top respect from any invading club. The Lords had their pride and would not drop their flag to pass through. So ever since then there has been a fight for respect, and now there are not too many clubs but a lot of gangs. By: Mr. Shonnovan, A.K.A. Demond

I typed his introduction, framed it with colored paper, and glued it to the center of a white paper. Demond drew gang symbols of both gangs on the white around the writing. It made a beautiful cover for our book.

Almost all of the boys belonged to a gang, and the members of a gang stuck together and helped each other while locked up. If a boy didn't belong to a gang he might pretend to belong, but if he didn't know enough of the signs to make the others believe his membership, they would go after him. If a boy admitted he did not belong to a gang, the others called him a neutron and ganged up on him.

Melvin wrote a poem that indicated he was doing some serious thinking about gangs.

WHAT'S A GANG?
A gang is a mob that sometimes robs
Cause they don't have jobs.

Chapter Nineteen

They want to be bad, not sad.
They have different names,
But there is not one who is in fame.
They need to realize we're all from the same gang
And we're at war with our own race.
We need to slow this pace,
Taking from each other and killing each other.
It's not going to get us a step further.

One day Tony and Devon were quietly talking, looking at a paper. The paper listed sixteen "Concepts," such as stealing, killing, breaking and entering, rape, cheating, and lying. As I looked it over, I asked, "You mean you're required to do these things?"

"Oh, no. There's supposed to be a NO in front of everything," Tony said. He hesitated, grinned, and looked surprised as he said, "You see, we're supposed to be good."

I developed a questionnaire concerning gangs and began interviewing one boy at a time. The students enjoyed the individual attention, especially since I recorded the interviews and they could listen to them later.

Below is an excerpt from the interview with Gary. He was more mature and well mannered than most of the boys. His responses show some of the changes that developed within gangs when the gang members began making great amounts of money selling drugs.

The guys loved to talk for the tape recorder and were quiet while someone was recording. They busied themselves with other activities while Gary pulled his chair up beside my desk. His black hair, about an inch long, framed his face. (A barber came regularly to the school to

Teachah Don't Know Nothin'

keep the boys' hair trimmed.) He wore the standard white t-shirt - his with an owl insignia - and the contrast with the white shirt made his black skin glisten. He leaned forward and put his forearms on the desk as he answered my questions.

INTERVIEW WITH GARY

Name of gang: BG, Black Gangsters.

How often do you have gang fights? We don't fight nobody, just make money. That's all we do, sell drugs. Don't fight nobody. Enough money for everybody.

Do you think BG's and Vice Lords could work together? No, it's not possible.

Tell me about girls in the gangs. We got girls in our group, but some don't. Some gangs are all-girl sets.

If a girl needs to be violated in your gang, how is that handled? They'll pick a girl off the board, whose got rank, and they'll violate the one that did something wrong. They hit her for two minutes and thirty seconds. One girl to one girl. It would hurt a lot. They body would be harmed in every place, the face, the body, and everywhere else. The person they doin' it to can't hit back.

When boys be violated, we hit everywhere and they can't do nothin', for one to three minutes. Sometimes it be so bad the boy die.

Do you know anything about the first leader of the group, how he was chosen?

He had to do serious crimes and he had to murder a couple of people and then he would be chosen for that higher position.

Chapter Nineteen

How do most of the people in your neighborhood feel about gangs? They love um. Oh, you talkin' about the neighbors and all? They sleep on it. They don't know nothin' about it, ya dig? We just be makin' money, we don't be shootin' nobody and jumpin' on nobody for no reason. We nationwide.

The neighbors don't know about it? In a way they know, but some of them sleeps the thang, you know, some of um mind they own business. And some of um, they just buy the drugs, you know. Ain't none of that trickin' thang. 'Cause we are New and Improved Black Gangsters.

What does that mean, new and improved? You know, we better now. Back then, we was slow. We wasn't on our money at first. We was gang bangin'. Now, we makin' money. We ain't gang bangin'. We ain't on none of that Black Gangster killin' or none of that junk, you know. We just make money and keep a low profile. We new and improved. We done got better. We come to jail by accident. Rather, I'm in jail by accident.

By accident, is that from drug dealing? Most likely. Either drug dealin' or a girl.

A girl? Yeah, you know, we have our feelings.

You mean you fight over a girl? They do, not me. I ain't fightin' over no girl.

You mean they will fight over a girl? Yeah, if it come down to it.

How many people in your neighborhood are taking the drugs? A lot of um.

Teachah Don't Know Nothin'

How do the police treat your gang? Man, they treat us like kings. They don't fuck with us. We know some of the polices, and you know, we be payin' um off. If some of them catch us, they be wantin' guns and stuff to let us go. That's why I say we new and improved, 'cause I'm not in here for no drugs. I'm in here for a mistake I made on my own. I accepted that IPS (Intensive Probation System) and violated it.

How do the teachers at school react to the gang? My school? At my school we don't gang bang. Don't nobody know nothin' about no New Breed. If you ask somebody have they heard about New Breed, they'll say no, what's a New Breed?

You're called a New Breed? Yeah. They don't even know what New Breed is, 'cause, you know, we stay undercover. We just make money. Now, you ask anybody in here what's a Breed is, and they'll go, I ain't never heard uv it. 'Cause, we makin' our money.

About how many people are in the New Breed? Thousands! Thousands!

And you're not getting into trouble or things like that? I'm tellin' you. No, you'd hear about it. Just trust me. I'm not sayin' we not gettin' in trouble, but it's not everywhere. People don't know nothin'.

How do your parents react to the gangs? My mother, she straight. She be tellin' me to git out and stuff, but you know, when it's done, it's done. I'm gonna do what I want to do regardless. So, she don't like it, but I do it.

Chapter Nineteen

How important are things like boys' clubs and things like that in your neighborhood? We own two pool halls, right there, and a little restaurant.

You mean the New Breed? Right. Yeah, we have our clubs.

Is your girlfriend involved with gangs? Hell, naw. I'd beat her ass. My woman is pregnant. Fo months pregnant. I'll have a baby in a little while.

Do you want your son to be in gangs? Hell, naw. I'll beat his little ass. I know I'm settin' a role model, but, man, hey, I was brought up like that. He ain't gonna be brought up like that.

If he's a boy, he's going to try to be like you. Yeah, I know, but you dig, when I get older, when I get up there, trust me, I know what time it is.

You mean you know when to get out? Right. And I know when to stop. That's a promise.

What does your girl think about you being in a gang? She can't stand it, 'cause I'm always outside, sellin' drugs, and you know she be worryin' about me. Like now, that's how I got in here, tryin' to go security for this nigger, and my IPS officer came and I watn't in the house, 'cause I had forgot all about it. That shit was goin' to my head.

What do you spend most of your time with the gangs doing? Sellin' drugs and goin' shopping, and that's it. No gang bangin', no shootin' nobody, no beatin' up nobody. No lie, either. Don't do nothin' unless it's necessary.

Teachah Don't Know Nothin'

How much money would you say you make a week? In a week? Me? I make about twelve hundred. And could a made more if just I was out there, you know, how long I was out there.

But it averaged out to be about twelve hundred? What did you do with the money? I spent it on me and my girlfriend shoppin'. And buy my mama somethin'. You know, I just spent it. If you see my girlfriend, you'll know what I did wid it. Trust me, I don't go changin' the shoes she got.

What about saving some for the future? Yeah, I know what you talkin' about. I got some money saved up right now. My mama gonna bring me some shoes tomorrah. Rather, I had already bought um for Easter.

About how much would you say you have saved? I got about - see, once I had got on IPS I watn't sellin' until about two months. So, I got about four hundred, three hundred dollars put up.

About three hundred put up. What are you going to do with that? When I was out I was spendin' it. I can't really save no money at this point. When I know I'm gonna be locked up, that's when I be workin', then just put the money up.

What about your child, wouldn't it be wise to save for him? I know what you sayin'. But, I ain't got to that point yet. I get off IPS in November. I shouldn't have that baby till about December, hopefully. I don't know when she s'posed to have it. But, anyway, I got that covered.

Chapter Nineteen

Was there a special thing that happened or some special reason you joined your gang? Yeah, I was a GD, right? I got jumped on, over a female. So, you dig, my cousin is the chief of all of um. So when I got jumped on, he was like, come on home, come on home, you dig? So I come on home. He took me shoppin', bought me clothes, and then he put me on the spot and I started makin' money. Within a week I made almost fifteen hundred dollars. And all I did was stand out there and looked out. And so you know, they blessed me and I came on home.

Was the fight you had over the girl you got pregnant? No, it was another girl I got pregnant. Rather, she say she got pregnant by me and she was one of the GD brothers and I was like I didn't get her pregnant. I told um I didn't get her pregnant so they jumped on me.

Did they want you to take care of the baby? It watn't mine! She be havin' it sometime this month or next month. I been sayin' it watn't mine, 'cause I was locked up all them other times. They probably would a got me if I watn't locked up.

Do you ever recruit guys? Yeah.

Where do you recruit? Everywhere. School, Audy Home, anywhere.

How do you recruit? Brother be up there talkin' about somebody in his gang treatin' him wrong, and we be like, come on home to the BG thang. They come home, start sayin' they BG. Takin' advantage, tellin' they brothers they BG. Man, from there, somebody

233

Teachah Don't Know Nothin'

jump on um, he still BG, Black Gangster. If he come around our crib, he be tooken care of. We look out for you. (He looked at the tape recorder.) I like this.
You like the interview? Yeah.
If you were to have a chance, in high school, to go to school in the morning and have breakfast, then go to classes to learn academics like reading, writing, history, and math. You have lunch, and after lunch go to a job where you could learn a skill, something you liked to do, where you could make a little money at the job while you learned, and work at it after you graduate to make money - how do you think that would work? You could even go back to school for supper if you wanted to, and there would be things to do at night - like art, music, dancing, computers, things you like. If you didn't have a place to go to sleep at home, you could stay at the school. How do you think that would work out? Would you like it? I would do it. I would do it in the position I'm in now. I don't want to get in no more trouble sellin' drugs. But, you know, at the age of sixteen, that's all I can do. At this point, when I got IPS, I'm tryin' my best to git a job. I'm goin' to school, too. I'm not doin' good in school, but I'm goin'. I'm tryin'. I'd like that real better. If you had a school like that you wouldn't need no gangs. Everybody'd go to school.

My final question evidenced the thinking I had been doing, trying to come up with some kind of solution for the kids - to help them want to stay in school, to provide some kind of training for productively earning a living, to give

Chapter Nineteen

them a chance to find meaning in their lives in a constructive environment.

For most of the Audy boys, the meaning in their lives came from gang association. When a boy joined a gang he received a new name - a nickname. One of the smartest boys, Shawndell, was nicknamed Kid Murder. I had bought a second-hand computer for the classroom, and Shawndell figured out how to use it. One day when he was showing me what he'd learned, he said, "I got plans. I'm trying to allocate all my plans toward being a better person."

"Don't you think you might need to change your name to fit the better person?"

"You right about that. But if I change nobody gonna know who I am. They gonna look up to me as Kid Murder."

"You're likely to get shot with that name."

"I got eyes in the back of my head. Ain't nobody gonna walk up on me. They might get a lucky shot, but they gonna be smellin' bad."

"Where do you think you'll be when you're twenty-five?"

"I'll probably be a professor by then."

"You still going to keep that nickname?"

"Like I said, everybody gonna still look up to me,' cause I'm Kid Murder. All my old allies gonna come up to me and say, 'What's up, Murder?'"

"Do you think you're really going to be a professor?"

"That's what I'm studying to be. I'm studying to improve my vocabulary, learn new words. I'll know what the words mean, not just trying to make my speech sound good."

Teachah Don't Know Nothin'

"When you get out of here, are you still going to gang bang?"

"When I get out, I still gotta take care of business, but I'm planning to settle down."

"How long do you think it'll take for you to settle down?"

'It ain't gonna be that long. Just take care of a little shit going down my way. Some people got killed, some people got shot, gonna take about three months. Gotta get everything straight, 'cause when I get out there, things is gonna turn. That's how I got that name, Kid Murder. Motherfuckers gonna be thinkin' twice about comin' at somebody, 'cause I'm the type that I'm gonna come right at um."

"What I'm concerned about is that before you get settled down and become a professor, you might get yourself killed, maybe because of that name."

"That's why I'm planning to move from my environment where I'm at. I could move to Hawaii or someplace."

"That would be a wise thing to do, move someplace where there are no gangs."

"Gangs everywhere."

"Shawndell, you have so much potential, you could do anything you want to do. What would you think if the judge would sentence you to someplace outside Chicago, like to a prep school?"

"I'd go. Shit, of course I'd go. I wouldn't be around no niggers trying to trap me, like if you don't stick up for yo sef, he gonna call you a pussy, everybody gonna call you a pussy and you gonna feel small. That's why you gotta defend yo sef and not let nobody call you out of your name.

Chapter Nineteen

If I was out of town I wouldn't have to worry about nobody comin' at me. I wouldn't be worryin' 'bout laying dead in a casket with niggers saying prayers over me and throwing a little dust on me, and holy water and all that."

Shawndell and I got interrupted. I didn't get a chance to ask him to tell me more about gang funerals, but here's an excerpt lifted from a recorded interview with another student that details a Gangster Disciples funeral:

> Right after the person is kilt, we have a get-together, and have a moment of silence. Then we get drunk and pour out half of every drink for him. In front of his house, they's a big stone with his name carved in it. We eat and drink, and throw food around the stone, put gasoline around the stone and burn it. That lasts for about half a hour.
>
> All G.D.s come to the funeral. We go to the casket all together and look inside. Each person gives a kiss on the forehead and throws up the fork (three fingers raised), and we put a joint up inside his jacket on his chest. We light another joint and everybody pull off of it then put the joint between his fingers till it burn down. When we sit down, the other gangs, the B.D.s and such, they come up there and they view the body. Then everybody go to the back and sit down until the funeral over, then go back up there and view the body one more time, and close the casket and pick it up and carry it out to the car. We wear our colors, the same colors that the person who got killed got on. At the burial, after everybody pray for him, the very last thing is, we all say the G.D. Law and the G.D. Prayer.

Teachah Don't Know Nothin'

Tony, one of the quiet boys, came over and put his arm around my shoulder and whispered, "I need you to write for me again today, but we have to do it quiet so nobody can hear." I went to my desk. Tony sat in a chair in front of the desk and said, "Write 'creed' there." I didn't understand what he said, and after a few attempts he said, "Forget that, just start there," and pointed to the first line.

Then he recited the creed for the Vice Lords. After each few words, he started at the beginning, reading with me the words I'd written, and added a few more. If another boy came close he stopped talking. When we finished he said, "Now at the bottom write. . .", and he started to say the meaning of the six points of the star. He couldn't quite remember, so he wrote the numbers one through six under each other, circled them, and told me what to write by each number.

When I finished, he picked up the paper and started to walk away. I said, "Will it be OK if I have a copy?"

He looked a little puzzled and said, "Why? You can't put it in the books."

"No, I know that. I'd like a copy for the book I'm writing about gangs."

That was all right, and he agreed that I could make a copy. I was glad to get it, for the meaning of the six points was different from the ones I had seen before. The guys had mentioned there were new meanings, and now my information had been updated. They also told me that once my book got published, they'd have to change all their literature, for it's supposed to be secret. As time went by, I learned that changes were made frequently. They changed

Chapter Nineteen

the "knowledge" just because they wanted to make a change, the same way bureaucratic agencies keep changing their structures with new terminology.

To quote Demond, "How can you summarize gangs? Senates are gangs. Governments are gangs. Election, that's a gang - he's pullin' rank."

Lenny told me his gang assignment was to go to school, get an education and become an attorney. The gang hadn't chosen wisely with him, for while he did work at his academic assignments, he didn't have the basic intelligence to become an attorney. I was becoming more aware that a kid with really low ability could not be an active participant in a gang. Not only did the gang members have to learn complicated "literature," they had to be aware of small signs of gang affiliation, such as hand signals, handshakes, nicknames, tatoos, how hats were turned, and greetings.

Jermaine was definitely bright enough to be a gang leader. Here's a poem he wrote that we posted on the bulletin board.

> MY LORD
> My Lord is a Lord who hears all my cries,
> My Lord is the Lord who saves people's lives.
> My Lord is a Lord that I know will always care
> So when I'm feeling down and out,
> I know He's always there.
> So put your fears in His hand,
> Do his will and obey his commands,
> A Lord can be as strong as you allow him to be.
> So love Him with all your heart
> So that your spirits will flow free.

Teachah Don't Know Nothin'

I liked the poem very much and was pleased that Jermaine had written such fine thoughts, especially the line about the Lord being as strong as we allow him to be, which seemed profound. He even drew a picture of a cross underneath, with a rose entwined on the cross. After the poem had been on the bulletin board for a long time, one of the boys informed me that it was a gang prayer and not religious at all. Lord, in Jermaine's lovely poem, referred to the gang leader.

A white boy called Doc came in his first day with his hair cut less than an inch all over his head and asked when the barber came next. I said, "With your hair that short and you still want a barber, you've got to be a Skin Head." "Tell me about Skin Heads. I don't know about them."

Shawn said to the class, "Might as well pull up your chairs, she's writin'."

Doc told me about the three types of Skin Heads, and differences between them. Before he stopped talking I had many pages of information about Skin Heads. Of course, *he* belonged to the one that was not prejudiced and was just for making this country better.

Chapter Twenty

Since windows in their rooms upstairs were small and near the ceiling, the only way the Audy boys could glimpse the outside world was by standing on their desks, and then they still couldn't see much. (Each room had a bed, a desk, a chair, and a toilet.) On the fifth floor they had access to a small, enclosed playground surrounded by high walls. For these reasons, the boys in my classroom often stood and looked out the big, low windows and I thought it important to allow for time there.

I sometimes watched their silhouettes at the windows. Most of them looked small and vulnerable.

Jamie stood looking out one day and said, "What's it like outside? Wind feel good when it blowing, don't it?"

John asked, "Is it hot outside today? I don't even know what fresh air smell like. The playground ain't fresh air, got walls all around."

Teachah Don't Know Nothin'

Shawn said, "After seven months in Audy, I forgot what it feel like to be on the bricks."

Antwon was sitting at his desk drawing. He said, "I been in here so long I forgot what a flame look like. How I gonna draw a flame when I don't know what it look like?" He lit a cigarette lighter and he looked at the flame and said, "OK, I'll put a little blue on it."

Jamie asked, "Can you turn on the radio? I got to get outside off my mind. I can't stand this."

It wasn't only the outside they missed. Shawn said, "It's been so long since I chewed some gum I don't remember what it's like. Maybe I'll chew a little paper. And I ain't seen no money in so long I forgot what it look like." He stood quietly for a minute, then said, "Look at all them free people out there. "

One afternoon a girl was standing on the sidewalk on Ogden Avenue in a tight, black, sleeveless low-cut pantsuit. She knew the guys were looking at her. Although they knew she couldn't hear them they said, "Turn around, let us see yo butt." She turned and they cheered.

When the boys moved away from the windows and settled down to work, David and Maurice began reading astrology books. I had included astrology books in our collection because the subject interested the kids enough to make them read. Maurice raised his head and said to me, "What that mean?"

"Read it again," I said. "I didn't hear you."

He read, stumbling over the words: "You are ir-re-sis-ti-ble."

Chapter Twenty

"Irresistible," I said, "means nobody can resist you - people like you." All the boys within hearing distance laughed.

Shawn said, "Let me read about me. I want to get to know myself."

David asked, "What uncontrollable mean?"

Shawn replied, "That's when you go off all the time."

Shawn's response made me curious. Though I was familiar with the term, I asked, "What does that mean, to go off?"

"You see," he explained, "that's when the wire that holds all the little marbles in your head that hold your brains together, just pops."

"You mean, when you go off, you can't control what you do?"

"That's right."

On the chalkboard we put each person's name with his sun sign. I noticed that when a boy read the characteristics listed for his sign, he might admit to some of the negative qualities mentioned, but it was the positive points he remembered and talked about later. A number of times that day Maurice said, "I'm irresistible." He seemed to be saying, I am an important, valuable person.

A little later when things were getting a bit hectic in class and I said, "You guys need to settle down. I think I'm getting ready to go off."

They all grinned. David said, "Ain't never seen nobody go off like that."

Teachah Don't Know Nothin'

Later that week Shawn, David, and Lamont were sitting at the table in the reading alcove, busily talking and laughing, unaware I was listening.

"Somebody gonna rob Mrs. Oglesby when she be on the street." That was David's voice.

Shawn laughed and said, "Rob Mrs. Oglesby? How you gonna rob Mrs. Oglesby? You put a gun in her face and say 'Stick um up' and she gonna say, 'What kind of a gun is that?'"

They all laughed. Then they were off, taking turns imagining what I might say, laughing at each remark:

"Where'd you get a gun like that?"
" I never saw a gun like that before."
"Is this a gang thing?"
" What gang do you belong to?"
" Show me the hand sign."
" Your gang got a Wall of Fame?"
"Who is your grandmother? Do I know her?"
"Got any tattoos? Let me see."
"Do you need money, or is this just for fun?"
"What is this, trying to rob an old woman like me?"
"I got a whole bag of jellybeans. Want some?"

Shawn finished it up. "First thing you know you helpin' her get all your knowledge. No, you can't rob Mrs. Oglesby."

The line about jellybeans referred to the 25-pound boxes of jellybeans that I bought at Evon Candy Outlet on 28th Street. For each page written I began giving the boys two jellybeans. Once Shawn brought a page of writing to me and when I handed him his two jellybeans, he laughed and

Chapter Twenty

said, "If I was on the street and you gave me just two jellybeans, I'd knock you down and take them all. Here I am, locked up in this jail, happy to get two jellybeans."

Tony heard him. "You shouldn't bring us nothin'. We jailbirds."

I made some new booklets, containing ten or twelve pages of lined paper, and told the kids if they wrote a story to fill the book I'd give them a bag of jellybeans and get permission from Mr. Franklin, the man in charge of the sections, for them to take the candy upstairs. The boys wanted to know how many jellybeans were in a bag and I guessed about a hundred. A voice at the back of the room said, "I'll work all day for a hundred jellybeans."

And they did work all day. That was Friday, and some of them said their jellybeans lasted all weekend. Some said they shared with other kids, but others said they ate all their candy the first night.

Often, I'd go around the room and give each of the boys three or four jellybeans when they were not expecting them. If they were noisy, they'd get quiet. If they were busy working, they'd smile and say thank you.

When we had a Latino kid in class and I heard the boys counting in Spanish, we began learning Spanish. I wrote numerals, one through ten, on the board in English and Spanish, and some simple words like the ones for "thank you," "you're welcome," "good morning," and "good-bye." I'd pass the jellybeans out while we counted in Spanish, and the boys would respond with *gracias* and I'd say *de nada*.

Lola, the teacher aide was from Mexico, and she and Mr. Ray decided it would be good to have a formal Spanish class. We tried it one day during the time Lola could be there, but in short order the boys were bored and restless. We learned Spanish incidentally all during the day.

Jellybean bribes worked well in many instances, but for some situations there was no help. One morning George came to the desk while the others were working. "I'm going to court tomorrow," he said. "How much time do you think they'll give me?"

I asked, "What are your charges?"

"Murder."

"Any witnesses?"

"Yes. And they got us all over this building. My two homeys are in different places here and my brother's in County."

"How did it happen?"

"He killed our chief, and I said to the two G.D.s, 'You gonna help me kill him?' When we found him he said, 'What's up?' - and I shot him and killed him. What do you think the judge will do?"

"The judge gave one guy here natural life," I said. "He was with some others who did a murder."

By this time the other students were listening. Devon said, "Natural life? Ain't no parole for that. What did he do?"

"He and his friends raped and killed a nurse and took her money."

"That's all? They only giving three to ten for murder now. My homey only got three years for murder and he'll just have to do half of it."

Chapter Twenty

Our talk wasn't helping George. His eyes were big with fear. When I first began working at Audy, not many kids there were charged with murder. Five years later, at the time of this conversation with George, murder charge was commonplace.

In a low voice that almost trembled George said, "I hope he lets me go. I don't like it in here."

Maurice spoke up loud from the back of the room. "They ain't gonna catch me again for some little thing like stealing a car. If I ever come back in here it's gonna be for murder."

Javon said, "When I kill somebody I like to use a gun so you don't see the blood."

Leroy said, bragging, "When I kill somebody I like to use a knife so you *can* see the blood. What's the use of killing somebody if you can't see the blood?"

Derrick looked at me with a twinkle in his eye. "Mrs. Oglesby, you ain't never popped nobody?"

I smiled, and shook my head.

Freddie - with *ie* on the end, not *y*, he emphasized - wore glasses and was short, dumpy, quiet, and very serious. He opened our book of raps and began pointing out errors, both in the original student writing and in my typing. The book contained raps the boys had written and ones they knew by heart. Raps are poetry or songs, set to a definite rhythm and beat, usually presenting a philosophical message of some kind, and extremely popular with the black guys. The rap Freddie was correcting was evidently

Teachah Don't Know Nothin'

one he knew well. It was long - two full, typewritten, single-spaced pages.

He attacked the editing with intense vigor, more enthusiasm than he'd shown about anything. For two weeks I worked with Freddie on the editing - getting the raps perfect, the way he wanted them. When he was released I hadn't completed the typing. He left his address with instructions to send him copies.

A few weeks later I looked up and saw Freddie coming in the door. "Freddie, what are you doing here?"

"I broke probation."

"How did you get in this classroom?" Kids were assigned according to space available and I knew I wasn't due to get a new student that day.

Freddie answered, "I told them I had work to do in here."

"Freddie, you'd better not tell me you got yourself locked up again so you can write raps."

He grinned and picked up the folder, sat down and went to work - writing raps.

I bought a few tapes of rap music that we played while we worked. One was playing when Freddie came to the desk. "Mrs. Oglesby, you like raps, don't you?"

"What makes you think that, Freddie?"

He smiled, "Watching yo feet with the music." I never could train my toes to be still when they heard music.

Freddie wrinkled his brow and asked, "You got a tape player in yo car?"

"Yes."

"What do you play on the way home when you leave your favorite rap tape here for us?"

Chapter Twenty

I told him I had other tapes to play and didn't tell him I only listened to raps at school.

A little later two boys pulled their desks to the back of the room and got noisy. I walked back to them and started asking questions.

"Is this school similar to your regular school? Can you think of ways we could make this class better? Do you have any ideas about how schools could better educate children?"

Both boys became serious, with facial expressions that told me they were thinking about my questions. Rob, the older one, said he knew we were not really educating the inner city kids. He said he thought they ought to learn to read and write and be able to do arithmetic. For things like science and social studies, kids could read only a couple of pages a day, so they wouldn't get bored. And kids should learn how to use tools - simple tools for the little kids.

No longer was he acting silly and disrupting the class. He had taken on a mature and thoughtful demeanor, honestly trying to find solutions for how to better educate children. As he talked I took notes- I was taking him seriously. I was continually amazed at the response when I asked for information and made that information valuable by recording it or taking notes. Often the kids' ideas proved helpful, and it was always easy to find questions to ask about things they knew more about than I did.

One night I dreamed I was in the classroom listening to the boys talking about how they committed their crimes,

Teachah Don't Know Nothin'

and some of the details of what they had to do as part of their gangs. I asked them how they learned so much and had become such experts with their crimes. "Oh, our leader taught us."

"And who is your leader?"

All hands pointed to a kid at the front of the room who was my best helper and could do almost anything, the one I was so thrilled to have in class.

I thought the dream was probably about Derrick. He ranked at the top on achievement tests, wrote beautiful poetry, drew lovely illustrations, was quiet and reserved, and worked well all the time. He did not enter into the gang talk and silly games with the others. He impressed me so favorably that I wrote a letter to his judge, and told the social worker how great he was. I remembered the dream when I walked by his desk and found him doing fabulous gang graffiti!

One of the quietest and most withdrawn of the students was a black boy named Devon. He showed little interest in anything. He overheard Shawn asking for help with a letter to the judge, and asked if he could write to the judge. It was letter-writing day, Friday. He wrote a long letter and came for help to get everything just right. He explained to the judge that he accidentally killed his best friend, Tyrone, with a gun. He said if the judge would let him out he would be a son to Tyrone's mother and help her the way Tyrone would have. He'd even go to schools and talk to kids about how dangerous it was to have a gun and what happened to

Chapter Twenty

him with his gun, and tell the kids they should do good things, not bad.

The next Friday Devon was writing again when Darnell grabbed his paper and began reading it, then started making fun of him - calling him a punk and saying he got raped in the Audy Home.

I said, "Darnell, bring that to me." I scan read the paper and saw that Devon had written that he had "got fucked in my ass by two niggas cause I didn't give them my food."

"Devon," I said, "did this really happen to you?"

He nodded.

"Did it happen here?"

Again he nodded.

To the class I said, " Have any of you ever been raped? Don't answer. Just think. Do you have any idea what emotional harm is done to anyone who gets raped?"

Anthony said, "You mean mental?"

"Yes, mental, emotional, and physical. Our bodies are private and personal, and being raped can hurt more than anything another person can do to us. You see rape is not really a sexual act. It's anger, hostility, violence, and a need for power."

Darnell asked, "Mrs. Oglesby, how come you know so much about rape. You ain't never been raped."

"No, I haven't, but I've known people who have been, and I saw how much they suffered. When you make fun of someone who's been raped, you add to the hurt."

Darnell raised his voice to an angry pitch and said, "I'd kill anybody who tried to rape me. I'd never let that happen to me. Only punks get raped."

Teachah Don't Know Nothin'

I said, "There are times when a person can't do anything. There may be more than one person to hold you down, or someone might hit you with something and knock you out. You can't always control such situations." The class silently returned to their work.

After a bit Devon brought his letter up for me to mail. He said, "Mrs. Oglesby, I'm really going to miss you." Again, as he was leaving for lunch, he said, "I'm really going to miss you. You know I'm going to kill myself today. Don't nobody care nothin' about me."

I immediately reported what Devon had said to Mr. Ray, the counselor. He laughed and jokingly repeated the common phrase, "So, the world would be better off if more of them killed themselves."

I didn't laugh. I handed him the letter that Darnell had grabbed from Devon.

> Dear Moosey,
>
> Yo, what up, nigga! What yo pussy ass been doing out there. Well, as for me I'm about to kill myself because I got fucked in my ass by two nigga's cause I didn't give 'em my food. So I hope you know I still love you but since I been fucked I feel like I got my man hood tooken so I can't live with knowing I'm a punk ass nigga!
>
> Love Always, Devon!

We didn't routinely screen the letters the boys wrote, but I felt like the circumstances warranted an invasion of Devon's privacy. I handed Mr. Ray the letter Devon had given me to mail.

Chapter Twenty

Dear Moosey, What's up with you bitch. You don't love me. You or Sal. Fuck both of yawl. You know I miss my mama. Fuck the world and my dad, and shit, I told god to take me away. Tell Sal she don't have to come to see me no more ever.

I won't be alive when she come. I am not saying this to make her come. Moosey, I am ready to dead. Man, Too told me don't worry. Moosey, I can't take it no more man, when I killed myself I know you ain't going to miss me but I don't give a fuck no more.

I talk to god ever night. I allways think about Tyrone, man (the friend he killed). I am about to go crazy in this mother fucker. I think if I killed myself it would be best for me. Don't tell nobody Moosey, OK? I want to be with my Mama, Rute, Tyrone,and Harrison. I don't have to get out now. I will be with my Mama and god forever. I cry ever night hoping I killed myself. Too can have my car if Too want it. I don't need shit now. I won't be alive. That's all I got to say, By bitch.

Mr. Ray left immediately to alert the staff upstairs and see that Devon got help. If the staff upstairs had known that Devon had been raped, he would not have come to class.

The kids were talking about their release dates, and what happened if their mothers didn't come for them. Because the boys were juveniles, the authorities couldn't release them except to the custody of a parent or guardian. Leroy said, "My O.G. (Old Girl, meaning mother) better come get

Teachah Don't Know Nothin'

me, that bitch. If she don't, they can only keep me seven days and then I'll beat her up. It's my house. I took it over. She do what I say."

From across the room I heard, "Don't matter what yo mother do to you, you don't never kill yo mother. Now, fathers, that's different."

Leroy's remark was unusual. The one from across the room was the more typical. When the Audy boys spoke of their mothers, they usually expressed love. Frank wrote the following poem. In it he expresses the sentiments I often heard.

>MOM
>
>Mom is the only one for you,
>Without her you would not be. Mom.
>When you get into trouble, who do you
>call? Mom.
>When you are sick, who takes care of you?
>Mom.
>Who's there when you need someone
>to talk to? Mom.
>When you've messed up in your life,
>Who's there to tell you to pick yourself
>up and start over? Mom.
>I know one thing my mom does that no
>other mom does,
>She takes all the shit I have done in
>my life, and loves me.
>But one thing my mom does not do
>is trust me any more,
>And I don't blame her.

Chapter Twenty

The boys thought their mothers should lie for them in court. Often I'd hear Mr. Ray say, "I'm not lying for you. I'm not your mother." Occasionally someone would ask if I'd lie for my boy if he was in trouble with the police. I'd always tell them "No, if I lied for him once, he might think he could get away with doing the same thing again. I'd want him to learn from what he'd done and take the consequences."

I often had the feeling that the boys thought of me more as a mother, grandmother or friend than as a teacher. One day the class was quiet and busy while David sat with his elbows on his desk, his head in his hands, looking at me. When he was sure he had my attention he asked, "Mrs. Oglesby, how come you work here?" Fifteen sets of eyes looked at me.

"What do you mean?"

"Ain't you afraid to work here?"

"I never thought about it."

"You married? That's how come you so happy? Ain't you got no husband and no kids to drive your crazy?"

I motioned for him to come to the desk, pushed aside some papers, and pointed to pictures under the plexiglass on the desk top. "These are my kids, two boys and two girls."

"Bet they ain't bad like the kids in here."

I said, "You think I like to be here?"

"You always be happy," David said. "Sometimes I try to make you mad but you don't get mad. And you got energy. Lots of energy."

"I like to work here. That gives me energy."

Teachah Don't Know Nothin'

"Do you get paid for working here?"

"Yes. Teachers get paid."

"You a teachah, just like in a real school?"

"This is a real school. A real school inside the detention center."

"How come yo kids let you work here?"

"I work where I want to work. My children understand."

"I wouldn't let my mothah work here, with kids like us. Just look at us, we bad kids, we criminals."

David pointed to my son Don's picture: reddish blond hair, blue eyes, and light complexion. He said, "You sho got yo sef a white boy there."

One morning I had a lot of copying to do and talked Mr. Ray into covering the class for me. The kids didn't like for me to be away. I was explaining that I would only be gone a short time when a big fella named Clarence said, "You know our Mama ain't gonna leave us for long."

Rob said, "She ain't our mama, she our grandmama. Dynamite Grandmama, that's what they call her upstairs."

We had some new students come into class that morning and Clarence said, "Tell them this is the best class in the school."

I did. I told them, "This is the best class in the school with the best students in the school."

Mr. O'Malley came in the next morning when Omar was playing a video game and yelled to me, "What are you doing with a video game? And what is he doing there first thing in the morning? This has got to stop!"

Chapter Twenty

He left the room before I could say anything. One of the guys said, "How come you let him talk to you like that and you didn't say nothin' back to him?"

I answered, "We need to be tolerant of Mr. O'Malley right now. He's just back from the hospital. He had a heart attack and his medication might make him irritable."

Omar turned from the video game and said, "You don't have to use such big words that we don't understand."

Mr. O'Malley came back immediately with Mr. Ray to stay with the kids so he and I could talk. We went into the prep room. He closed the door and said he didn't think it was fair for me to have games and so many things in my room when other teachers didn't. I told him they could provide them as I did. Then I explained to him the benefits of having the video game. Some kids who couldn't do anything well could play a video game well. One guy who could do almost nothing academically could get the game to work when no one else in the room could and gained admiration from the others.

I explained that Omar, who had been using the game that morning, had been extremely difficult to interest in any academic work or to conform to class rules, and the day before had worked hard all day with all his assignments. He was playing the game early because I was showing him I was pleased with his work and behavior. I was consciously using the video games with definite purposes in mind, not just for babysitting.

To my relief, Mr. O'Malley agreed. We went back into the classroom and he told the kids they were lucky to have a teacher like Mrs. Oglesby who explained the benefits of video games. When he told the kids we could keep the games, they clapped and cheered.

Later that day I looked around the classroom. Several kids were trying to get a video game to work, a few were making flash cards for learning Spanish. Some were recording the Black National Anthem on a tape recorder while others were watching a film. One boy was playing music on the keyboard, another typing a letter. The room was noisy, but all the kids were busily involved with activities important to them. This was the class I had pictured in my dreams.

My feelings about the class were somewhat verified by Mr. O'Malley, who came in one afternoon for the yearly teacher observation for the teacher evaluation report. Usually he came in for a few minutes and left. This time he stayed the whole afternoon. As he walked toward the door, he said, "Mrs. Oglesby, I would like to be a student in your class." I think I never received a compliment I appreciated more.

Though the kids had been arrested for criminal activities, and almost all the inner city kids I had worked with came from a violent and chaotic culture, twenty years of getting to know them had proven to me that they were no different than other kids.

They laughed and cried. They loved and wanted to be loved. They wanted to please and gain respect from adults and their friends. They wanted a good life for their families. And, when they were interested in an activity, they became enthusiastic and worked hard.

Chapter Twenty

I believe that each child is born with a gift for the world, and each one has to discover that gift. No one else can identify it - the discovery must be a personal one.

I wanted the various activities in my beautiful yellow classroom to provide the musical or technical or whatever other experiences a student needed on that journey toward self-discovery.

As I looked around the room I was elated, but underneath I could feel the sadness of reality: even if these students identified their skills and abilities, there wouldn't be much chance they could achieve their goals. If they could escape the culture, they would still be carrying the emotional difficulties that result from such an environment. Some do get out. Why? How? Perhaps some adult believes in them enough to cause them to believe in themselves enough that they can succeed without crime or welfare.

When I think of what can be done to help the inner-city children, my high school class motto pops in my mind. That motto hovers over my head and has all these years. "So little done, so much to do."

Acknowledgments

So many people helped me along the way toward the writing and completion of this manuscript that it is impossible to name them all. I hope those who might have not been recognized here know that I have not intentionally left them out and appreciate their efforts.

Flora Rodriquez-Brown, Professor, University of Illinois at Chicago, served as my mentor; affirmed my efforts, and opened many doors.

I thank Arpad Lengyel, Scientist, Dept. of Energy, for his encouragement and support.

Richard Duran, Professor, Graduate School of Education and Director of the Linguistic Minority Research Project at the University of California at Santa Barbara, visited and talked with my classes, and invited me to Santa Barbara to speak to his graduate education classes and Linguistic Minority Research Conference.

Dolores Kohl, CEO OF Kohl Educational Foundation, Founder, Kohl Children's Museum in Wilmette, IL, Founder of Kohl/McCormack Teaching Awards, a great friend, visited my classroom, read the kids' stories, and was always encouraging and supportive.

Victor Leo Walker, University of California at Santa Barbara, Research Coordinator for Afro-American Studies, visited my classroom and did linguistic research with my students.

Rachel Stine, who worked with me through countless hours of editing and typing stories, especially the ghetto-slang dictionary.

Leigh Garrison, M.A. Clinical Psychology, who counseled the children and me and offered helpful suggestions

Eileen McIntyre Colts-Tegg, who loved the stories about the children and did an interview with me on National Public Radio.

Barbara Lawing, editor, worked tirelessly to help organize and revise.

Branda Carl, who questioned and analyzed.

My writing group members, especially Tom Perkins, whose encouraging comments pushed me to complete the book; also Krista Sipe, Charles Alley, Lynn Dausman, Martha Simmons, Susan Lawson, Vanessa Schmieder, Sandra Cobb, and Richard Coffman.

Lucy Saxman, for suggestions and encouragement.

Teachers and administrators in all the schools, including Frank Tobin, John Hahn, Tom O'Malley, Jerry Archie, David Ray, Helen Pandya, Margot Gillin, Lola Navarro, E.

Coyne, Francis Conroy, Frank Martin, Jean Herron, Daniel Breen, Vivian Fenchel, Janet Dechter, Alberta Winters, and Michael Catania, Barbara Williams.

I also want to thank my children: John, Don, Samantha, Marianne, and Cary.

Denise Marchionda, ABPC editor, who helped especially with focus and elimination of material not pertinent to that focus. My mother, whose methods of discipline I used unconsciously in my classrooms.

My sisters, Ethel Wyant and Mary Stewart, who took my place feeding our mother the last two months of her life, so I could complete this book.

About the Author

When Dee Oglesby was a ninth grader she told her principal she didn't like school, that if she were old enough and her mother would let her, she'd quit. That ninth grader would have been surprised to learn she would be going to school all her life. After earning a degree in education from National College for Christian Workers in Kansas City, and an M.S. from Northern Illinois University, Dee continued to go to school to get certified to teach in special areas. She studied at the University of Illinois at Chicago, Anderson College, Bradley University, University of Colorado, National College of Education and North Eastern Illinois University.

Her teaching career was even more varied than her education. Beginning with nursery school, she taught all grade levels through junior college, and worked as a reading consultant in various special education programs. For ten years she taught in schools in the northwest Chicago suburbs of Arlington Heights and Palatine. The last twenty years of her career she taught in Chicago's inner city schools. She was recipient of the Dolores Kohl International Teaching Award in 1989.

She also got certified to sell real estate and insurance. Those ventures were no more successful than the fly-in hunting and fishing lodge she and her husband operated in Ontario. It finally became clear to her that teaching was her destiny. She lives in Concord, North Carolina.

Everett Library Queens University
1900 Selwyn Ave., Charlotte, NC 28274